THE
WOMEN'S
MOVEMENT

THE WOMEN'S MOVEMENT

Social and Psychological Perspectives

Edited for the American Orthopsychiatric Association
by Helen Wortis and Clara Rabinowitz

A Halsted Press Book

JOHN WILEY & SONS, Inc.
New York – Sydney – Toronto

First edition published in 1972
   by AMS Press, New York.
   Second Printing, 1973
First paperback edition published in 1972
   by Halsted Press,
   a Division of John Wiley & Sons, Inc., New York
   Second paperback printing, 1974

Library of Congress Cataloging in Publication Data

Wortis, Helen, comp.
   The Women's Movement

   Bibliography: p.
   1. Woman — History and condition of women — Addresses, essays,
lectures. 2. Women's Liberation Movement — Addresses, essays, lectures. 3. Woman — Psychology — Addresses, essays, lectures. I. Rabinowitz, Clara, joint comp. II. Title.
HQ1426.W67   301.41'2   72-6125
ISBN 0-404-10520-3
ISBN 0-470-96165-1 (pbk.)

Manufactured in the United States of America

TABLE
OF
CONTENTS

THE
AMERICAN
ORTHOPSYCHIATRIC
ASSOCIATION

The American Orthopsychiatric Association, founded in 1924, brings together 3550 anthropologists, educators, lawyers, physicians, psychiatrists, psychologists, nurses, social workers and sociologists in a collaborative approach to the understanding and treatment of mental health problems.

Uniquely *problem-centered*, the Association has pioneered and continues to stimulate the cross-fertilization of knowledge to broaden the horizons of the related professions. It has encouraged the breakthrough to valuable new theories based on expanded frontiers of research, leading to continued experimentation with new treatment programs.

The Constitution and Bylaws state these Purposes: "To unite and provide a common meeting ground for those engaged in the study and treatment of problems of human behavior.

"To foster research and spread information concerning scientific work in the field of human behavior, including all forms of abnormal behavior."

Orthopsychiatry as a term was derived from the Greek *ortho*, meaning straight, for two purposes: 1) to straighten out or to intervene before serious malfunction occurs and 2) to get straight thinking in psychiatry – an understanding of human behavior as an integration of the psyche in its interaction with the environment. This ultimately leads to the current concept of multidisciplinary treatment which is today a respected keystone in theory and practice. In recent years, Association task forces have worked on problems of 1) the crisis growing out of proposed cutbacks in appropriations for delivery of health care services; 2) the procedures for investigating prospective appointees for scientific advisory groups in the Department of HEW; 3) standards of health care offered Vietnam veterans by the Veterans Administration; 4) juvenile delinquency.

Membership has grown dramatically from 9 founding psychiatrists to the current roster of 3550. There are 1083 psychiatrists, 781 psychologists, 1171 social workers and 515 other professionals in related fields collaborating as AOA members. They live in 49 states, the District of Columbia, the Virgin Islands and 19 foreign countries. Standards of admission have always been high and inevitably must remain so. Qualifications for membership have been recently broadened to include workers and students in the mental health field who were previously not eligible. Details of qualifications and application blanks are available on request.

The Annual Meeting, held each year since 1924, is the Association's principal forum and climaxes a year of membership activity. It provides an exciting and stimulating opportunity for first-hand exchange of new ideas and experiences. Washington, D. C., New York and San Francisco rotate as host cities. New York is the site of the 1973 Meeting. The 7,000 to 10,000 participants come from universities, child guidance clinics, hospitals, schools, courts and many other public and private agencies. A theme focusing on a specific area of immediate concern is selected. Experts in this area are invited to promote awareness of the problem and to encourage those attending to explore their own potential roles and contributions.

Five Councils of the Association have been established by the Board of Directors to consolidate year-round membership activity in key areas. Councils will create task forces and study groups to give attention to specific mental health problems, within a specified time period. Councils' areas of functioning are: Administration, Research and Clinical Services, Human Rights and Minority Issues, Children and Youth Issues, Social Issues.

The American Journal of Orthopsychiatry, a quarterly scientific journal, publishes reports of significant activity and new theory in the field of human behavior, with particular attention to the multidisciplinary approach. Published papers are selected both from those presented at the Association's annual meeting and from those submitted directly to the Editor. A special fifth issue publishes digests of papers presented at the AOA annual meeting.

Published by the Association since 1930, the Journal has made strong impact as a highly respected source of current findings in research and therapy. Editorial attention is devoted to relevant issues and problems; significant literature is reviewed; new laws and governmental activity in the field are reported. There are more than 9,000 subscribers all over the world.

This book originated as a special section in Volume 41 of the *American Journal of Orthopsychiatry.* Most of the authors have revised their papers for this book which also includes new material, notably the resources bibliography and Margaret Mead's foreword, which did not appear in the *Journal.*

Charles H. King
President

FOREWORD

This is a clear responsible examination of some of the emerging trends in the Women's Movement which flared into being in the 1960s in the United States. The chapters are all by women, the tone is personal, but neither vituperative nor shrill, the demands for change and the laments for past sins involve no breast beating, and where men have been at fault, they are not unduly lambasted.

Written from within the disciplines of the behavioral sciences and designed originally as a special section for the *American Journal of Orthopsychiatry*, the emphasis is upon the needs and well being of the individual; the approach is developmental; the scrutiny for past sins includes criticisms of approaches in the behavioral sciences that seem, in the light of today's hopes and ideals, to have been misguided or downright wrong. So some of Freud's views of women's psychology and Bowlby's insistence upon the necessity for the continuous presence of the biological mother are both examined and repudiated as doctrines that have done harm. Perhaps the extent of the harm may have been exaggerated a little; by the time that Freud's view of women's passivity reaches the home of a working man's wife, it is pretty thoroughly diluted by other cultural influences. Bowlby's insistence upon the absolute necessity for the biological mother's caring for her children affected a small section of society, mainly the upper middle class, and coincided conveniently with the disappearance of servants and the appearance of modern labor saving devices, which between them, in most advanced industrialized countries, resulted in confining educated young women with children to the home. There are also convenient elisions made possible because the book is so contemporary. So changed attitudes towards sex are represented as the gross shift from Victorianism, when women were expected to be passive and passionless, to the present acceptance that women, and especially women as they become mature, are capable of positive enjoyment of sex. The steps in between, also related to the influence of Freud (which demanded a masculine type of orgasm from women and branded them as immature or neurotic if they failed to achieve it, so that a couple of generations of women were harried by inappropriate demands), is left out of the reckoning. So also is the importance of the belief that started in the 1920s that a life of active heterosexuality was the only normal life. Previously, belief in the possibility of life without active sex expression had provided protections for the spinster and the bachelor, and permitted latent homophiles to live dignified lives; parents to demand that their children become economically responsible before they became parents; and religious orders that were based on celibacy to preserve their integrity. All these earlier attitudes towards sex, together with the double standard, had crumbled away before the present women's movement and Masters and Johnson's research came along.

The keynote of this volume is here and now; the emphasis is contemporaneous and egalitarian. Wherever women in any way differ from men, and it is assumed throughout that women will continue to bear and rear children — with more and more help from men, as individuals, or federal, state and local governments — there is a demand that society should make up for the difference. The view of equality is, therefore, that anything in women's biological nature which prevents her from having full expression outside the home — in a public world in which men are tacitly assumed to be having a fine expressive time, free to come and go, engaged in business and professions of their own choosing — should be compensated for. And there is an expressed faith that men will be free of the pressures that dissatisfied wives exert upon them, subtly undermining their manhood and their faith in themselves as revenge for their own frustrated aspirations. Children too will be better off, if their mothers and fathers can treat each other as equally independent and complete persons, and face out their differences in honest confrontation without one being dependent and so using covert weapons, and the other using weapons of superordinate status and greater economic resources.

The American contributors to this volume have each written an essay on some aspect of the problem: they wrote independently and their views were not submitted to any discussion in a symposium. Their homogeneity and general agreement must thus be set down to the framework of Orthopsychiatry itself — a multi-disciplinary approach with the well-being of the individual at the center — as well as to the present climate of opinion among educated women in the United States. It is only necessary to contrast the general degree of agreement among the American writers with Mrs. Linnér's presentation of the Swedish approach — of which she is able to give us a single comprehensive picture — to see that the Swedish approach is also focused primarily on the issue of equality. This is so, although the Swedish reformists have explicitly directed their attention to the equality of sex roles for both sexes, while the American approach deals rather with making women more equal to men by reducing (and supplementing) the present homemaking role of women. There is, however, no such explicit American acceptance of the possible role of the house husband, as that contained in Swedish social provisions. Also, there is far less emphasis on social provisions in the approach of these American behavioral scientists. It is tacitly assumed that what is wrong is the expectations of sex roles found among men and women — and psychiatrists and educators — and that if these are corrected, the necessary arrangements — for equal pay, equal opportunity, maternity leave, day care — will all follow. The disastrous role of the suburbs on the division of labor between women and men, where men were absent all day, and women left without any help to rear their children, in isolation from relatives, friends, neighbors, or servants, is hardly mentioned. In contrast, the Swedes have set about their educational tasks by a continuous debate on social measures, social measures which, unlike the controversy over day care in the United States, seem to have united rather than divided different classes in Sweden.

This is a book, therefore, primarily for those who are concerned with practice involving individuals. It is for the mental health professionals, the psychiatrists, the family planners, the educators who have a central focus on personality. This is a book that provides a context within which the older members of the profession, whose main interest was not equality between the sexes but preparation of boys and girls for the roles they were expected to play, can repent, as Dr. Spock has been asked to do. Every family counselor who is about to help a wife adjust to the responsibilities and frustrations of contemporary suburban life, will be put on notice that instead he should see her as unfairly confined to wifehood and motherhood, and encourage her desire to escape — and assure her that, although it will be rough, her husband and marriage will profit by it. Single women may be encouraged to develop a life style of their own, and a life style to which the unhappily married may well aspire. Boys and girls are to be counselled to aspire equally to all professions because what differences there once were between the sexes — a long succession of pregnancies for women and a demand for great physical strength for the men — are both things of the past. The hostility that women and sometimes men display today, in situations where counselling is demanded, is now to be put down to their being an oppressed group, unfairly deprived of their rights, and suffering as all oppressed groups do from the poison of unequal relationships when such relationships should be equal. And there is a hopeful note, that human beings will then be able to deal much more competently with those situations in which there is genuine inequality, between parent and young child, teacher and pupil.

The more dramatic problems of the Women's Movement, the contrast between the fate of black women, already fully able to work and now faced with the task of establishing role relationships which may borrow too much from white middle-class standards, and the extreme positions of those who would repudiate men almost altogether, are deftly dealt with, not by chapters but as book reviews.

This is not a book that will end controversy, nor is it a book that will arouse violent partisanship. Rather the reader may be led on; to explore the past, other times, and other countries; the present, and the larger social economic framework within which we live; and the future, with more attention to such amenities as communities planned with neighborhoods where grandparents can play a part in the care of children, and education that does more about individual gifts and tempermental differences and does not merely prohibit telling girls to learn typing or study literature.

There are many unexplored areas of our present beliefs and practices about being human — especially about the role that biological sex plays in the lives in men and women — which deserve attention. Pushing child bearing and child rearing into the background, dismissing it as only part of life and one that will not be very onerous if the husband and state do their part, is only part of the answer.

Perhaps some of the younger readers will want to know what happened in the 1930s and 1940s that interrupted a movement toward just the kind of relationship between the sexes that is being pled for and heralded in this collection of articles. Women did have a full chance at education, the doors of the professions were opening, there was contraception that, although neither as convenient nor as easy to manage as the Pill, also did not have the pill's anxiety arousing possibilities; young men and young women shared together aspirations for individual creative work; there was no compulsion to have large families or even to have children at all; and child birth and marriage could both be postponed with far less anxiety than in the 1950s. And it went for naught. By the 1950s, the girls with the same education and the same economic position were clamoring to get into the home, desperate at the fear of being left out of the only kind of life worth living, with an overriding preoccupation with the production and rearing of children — at any price, to themselves and the overworked young husbands who rushed home to supplement their homemaking labors at night and on week-ends. There had been no new revelations in psychoanalytic theory and there was no new philosophical or theoretical justification for the regression. Yet it occurred, and those who share the hopes and aspirations of the authors of this volume may want to ask why. Perhaps equality and compensation for the "handicaps" of being a woman is not enough.

Margaret Mead

American Museum of Natural History
New York, New York
May 3, 1972.

INTRODUCTION

Within the last two hundred years, human society has changed more than in previous ones. While the rapid transition from an essentially rural, handicraft culture to the urban world of technology has affected every level of human social organization, women in particular have been enormously affected by these changes. The child-bearing function that patterned women's existence since the beginning of history no longer plays such a critical role in the lives of millions of women. One reason is that in technically advanced societies child-birth is not usually a life-endangering experience, so that women's life expectancy has been lengthened and her social role altered. Moreover, child bearing has diminished in social value in such societies, and most new-born infants can be expected to live to maturity. Most important, for the first time human conception can be controlled and reproduction planned.

All this has had profound effects upon society. We are witnessing great shifts in the concepts of marriage, of family, and of sexual role. Marriage patterns are changing and new forms of family structure are emerging. Work roles, formerly based upon sex, have become increasingly interchangeable between men and women, while education and socialization of young children is no longer assigned exclusively to the biologic parent. Under these circumstances, the self-concept of men and women must alter.

These and other changes in women's social role find their intellectual expression today in the women's liberation movement, just as in earlier periods the feminist and suffragette movements were expressions of changing female consciousness in, their time. It is a movement that found its first written expression in the 18th century with Mary Wollstonecraft's demand for citizen status, changing its demands and methods with changing times and needs. The present women's movement differs from the past in that it rejects equalitarianism with men as a goal and is largely indifferent to civic reform. The emphasis is now placed on basic revolutionary social change and upon a philosophic re-examination of the entire social structure and its goals.

It should be pointed out that no single political platform or methodology for such change has emerged and that "Women's Liberation" is a broad title covering many different points of view. Those involved agree, however, on the need for re-examining social concepts that until now have been assumed to have the validity of proven scientific fact. Thus, this book is concerned with some issues of the women's liberation movement and with a discussion of behavior theory from the point of view of this movement.

If you are willing to disregard the rhetoric and invective that characterizes some of its proponents, you will find, as we did, that the concepts deriving out of the radical women's movement are mind stretching. From this point of reference, many ideas that seemed unchangeable do, in fact, change. "Facts" prove not to be facts at all but systems of thinking that, though based on inappropriate methods of observation, have gradually gained social sanction.

Among the contributions that follow, those by social scientists delineate some of the changes taking place; those written by behavioral scientists indicate that the philosophic systems produced in a male-dominated society will show their bias upon analysis, but that these systems are slower to change.

We believe that members of the American Orthopsychiatric Association and others in the fields of mental health, devoted to the concepts and experience of change within the human personality, will find some of the circumstances and conditions of change in the making explored, and their own consciousnesses expanded, by the material presented.

Helen Wortis
Clara Rabinowitz

SOME EVOLUTIONARY ASPECTS OF HUMAN GENDER

Ethel Tobach

The word *gender* is a grammatical device for attributing sex to entities that have no biological sex. For example, gender is assigned to such phenomena as the moon, oceans, and hurricanes, or to occupations. It is used here to focus on the practice of assigning gender to human roles, presumably on the basis of biological sex. Actually, this assignment is an extension of societally determined roles. The extension is then justified as a reflection of the evolutionarily fixed functions resulting from inherited structures. This article will attempt to clarify the biological meaning of sex and differentiate it from societally assigned gender, in the context of this book. The subject is exceedingly complex and requires more time and space than is given here; accordingly, this article only deals with the most salient issues.

The fundamental differences in the biochemistry of the reproductive systems of the different sexes are related to the biochemical differences of the genes. Because gene action operates at the earliest stages of development, beginning with the formation of the sperm or egg, or the first structures of the new organism, these biochemical differences affect most of the physiological systems and structures that develop. Development of the new organism involves the fusion of three processes: growth, experience, and maturation.(3,4) Gene action is part of the experience of the individual, as experience is defined by Schneirla. In his theory, experience is any and all stimuli that affect the organism, whether the source of these stimuli are internal or external.

Although in both plant and animal forms, some species reproduce asexually – by splitting in half after a certain stage of development, as in amoeba; by forming a new organism from one part of another, as in the budding of *Hydra*; or by parthenogenesis, in which an egg produces a new organism without fertilization by the sperm, such as the rotifer, another invertebrate – the dominant means of reproduction involves the contribution of genetic material from different animals, or sexual reproduction. Sometimes it is difficult to assign *sex* (maleness or femaleness) to an organism, as in the case of yeast cells. Two groups of yeast cells can be clearly distinguished from each other in respect to their biochemistry and mating patterns. A hormone from one group will expand a cell from the other group, and *vice versa*, but the two hormones are not the same as the familiar estrogen and androgen that are usually associated with *sex*.(5)

The association of biochemical characteristics with different body-forms (dimorphism) exists at the earliest phyletic level, the acellular or one-celled organism level (protista). Sexual dimorphic variation is expressed in more specialized and differentiated forms and functions in the more complex species, but the effect of this variation is the same in all species. In sexual reproduction, regardless of species, there is usually a differentiated gonad for each sex, each one producing a sperm or egg. Many species are hermaphroditic, that is, the individuals of the species have both types of gonads, either concurrently or sequentially. Sexual reproduction produces a wider variety of individuals within one species than does asexual reproduction, because of the association of different biochemical characteristics with the different sexes. It is widely believed that the diversity produced by combining genetic material from two or more individuals played an important role in the evolution of species: Nonetheless, it is also true that species that reproduce asexually have also survived. The evolutionary process of natural selection has resulted in a diversity of modes of reproduction. Some questions remain: Why do only females reproduce parthenogenetically? Why cannot two individuals of the same sex produce a new organism?

It is possible to define the reproductive process by its three aspects: fertilization, incubation and nurturance. The diversity of modes of reproduction is exceeded by the diversity of behavioral patterns by which the three activities are carried out. The parts played by the male and the female in the three aspects of reproduction vary considerably from species to species. Fertilization of the egg by the sperm (formation of the zygote) may take place within the body of the organism producing the sperm or in the body producing the egg, or outside both bodies. It may result from the approach of the female to the male, or the male to the female.

Incubation, during which the zygote grows and develops, may take place within one or another of the parents; in a setting that is more or less structured by one or both parents, or in the typical environment of the species without any specialized modification of the environment, as when turtles dig holes in which eggs are laid. The offspring may be most dependent on the parents or other adults for survival (altricial state), or rather independent (precocial state) after emergence. Nurturance may be carried out by the male, the female, or both. Although feeding and thermal protection play a role in the development of normal sexual behavior, other socialization experiences are relatively important, depending upon the plasticity and complexity of the species.

Among invertebrates, incubation and nurture are most likely to take place outside the bodies of the parents. Occasionally, the external environment is modified to provide a setting that promotes growth and development, although the parents are no longer present. Outstanding exceptions to this pattern occur in the social insects, such as bees and ants. In these species, through the process of reciprocal stimulation, including nurturance activities, interindividual bonds are formed between adults and immature individuals, which promote the development of the offspring and lead to complex social organizations.(2)

Among vertebrates, the complexity and diversity of patterns of incubation and nurturance increase considerably. Among bony fish, males or females may carry developing embryos in their mouths. Once the young emerge and swim off, they are not dependent on the adults for nurturance. Amphibia most frequently deposit fertilized eggs that hatch into larval forms and later metamorphose into adults. These developmental stages take place independently of the activity of the adults, except in regard to the original deposition of the eggs. Among birds, the patterns of incubation vary from the laying of eggs in environments with appropriate temperatures, but not in nests containing eggs that one or both of the parent birds brood. The young are born at different levels of dependence on the adults. Mammals, both marsupials and placentals, are characterized by internal fertilization, but the degree of incubation also varies in this class as well, resulting in extreme altriciality, as in marsupials, to extreme precocity, as in the guinea pig, a placental mammal. Mammalian patterns of nurturance also vary, although the prevalence of significantly long periods of parent-young relationship is greater in this class of vertebrates than in any other.

Upon reaching the adult stage, the individual organizes its life space in regard to predators, feeding, interaction with conspecifics, and so forth, in accordance with the volutionary history of the species, and in accordance with the history of the individual. The reproductive activities of the individual are integrated with other patterns of behavior: there may be temporary cessation of feeding during incubation, as in the case of some birds and fish. In some species, as in the penguin, incubation is shifted from one parent to another as they engage in feeding in alternating periods. Some hawks bring the prey back to the nest where the other parent is brooding, so that both parents feed during incubation. Comparable variety exists among mammals. Some rodent and ungulate females feed themselves while nursing the offspring. In other complex social groups, such as wolves and wild cats, nurturing females and males in the group feed as part of a more complex socially organized pattern of activity. Among most primates, gestating and nursing females engage in feeding and movement through the home range along with the entire group. In many mammalian species, and particularly among primates, social groups are sufficiently organized to involve males in continual interaction with offspring. These interactions usually do not involve feeding of offspring, but are of a grooming and chasing-cuffing character, which is exhibited by adult females as well.

The variability of behavioral patterns in relation to reproductive processes makes it difficult to generalize about the gender of the role of individuals in other than mating behavior. In view of the variety of patterns on any one phyletic level, only the grossest hierarchical ordering of behavior is possible. Generally speaking, below the human level, the importance of environmental manipulation to provide settings for nurturance appears to decrease as the degree of behavioral plasticity increases. The young of primates are not maintained in special nests or settings. Rather, their environment is a social setting in which the offspring are usually firmly attached to the nursing female, either by clinging or, as it grows, by remaining close to the female. In the most highly socialized primate, the human being, one finds a new emphasis again on environmental manipulation to provide protective nurturance. Depending on the society in which the parent-young relationship occurs, the human infant is maintained in complex social environments for varying lengths of time, more or less in the proximity of the physiological mother, or another female adult, who may or may not nurse.

It is also possible to state generally that, among the classes of vertebrates, the mammals are most likely to nurture their offspring longer than other classes. Again, the human infant is nurtured the longest among primates, but depending on the society, the relationship between the child and its parents is more or less direct and immediate during this period. In many hunting societies, depending on whether the child is still nursing, it may be fed by its physiological mother, or by members of an extension of the original parturitional unit. The extension is sometimes large enough to include the entire tribe or clan. Or, in some forms of social organization such as the kolhoz or kibbutz, the nurturance of children is socially organized and participated in by many adults, with the women usually taking the leading role.

In comparing species-typical patterns of fertilization, incubation, and nurturance, it becomes apparent that with the consideration of human behavior, a new factor is introduced. In discussing birds or insects, it is possible to characterize the social organization of the species in a relatively static, generalized fashion. The changes that a particular species has gone through in evolution are not immediately apparent and must be analyzed by sophisticated behavioral studies. The temporal characteristics of such investigations are necessarily contemporary and too short to permit an "on-site" study of the evolution of social organization in one species. In analyzing these same patterns in human beings, however, with the exception of the prehistoric hominds and human beings, it is necessary to introduce the concept of societal change and its attendant concept of the changing role of the individual in different societies.

Throughout the animal world, the levels of social organization(6) can be ordered in terms of increasing complexity of social bond formation as a function of increasing plasticity of neural organization. In simpler species with limited potential for integrating experience, bonds are restricted to immediate stimulus conditions and contemporary hormonal and other internal states. As the interrelationship between hormonal and neural systems becomes dominated by the capacity of the nervous system to store and integrate past experience, the character of social organization becomes extended in time and differentiated among individuals. The complexity of social relationships increases. Although on all levels of behavioral and social integration, the substrate of physiological processes is present and evident, the operation of those processes in social behavior becomes more and more modified. Social experience begins to have profound effects on many aspects of physiological function, including reproduction. Mammals, and particularly primates, reared in conditions of social deprivation are unable to perform species-typical adaptive behavior leading to fertilization, incubation, and nurturance activity.(1)

On the human level, the substrate of biochemical and physiological processes is also present. The sexual dimorphism evidenced in fundamental biochemical processes, such as genes, persists and is expressed in both structure and function. In the complex social organization of the human, however, the dominance of societal factors becomes most patent. The physiological processes of fertilization and incubation, although the same in all societies, take place in social settings that vary historically, leading to damage, death, or survival of the foetus. In any one period of history, the supportive or destructive conditions in which fertilization and incubation take place vary with the class or social group to which the adults belong. Nurturance is accomplished by widely diversified procedures, depending on the society and the group within the society to which the child and parents belong. *It is no longer easy to generalize about the three processes as they occur in a particular species.* The physiology of reproduction in people is comparable in all settings. Different societal settings increase or decrease the probability of the survival of the offspring, as well as behavioral patterns involved in reproduction. It is possible that with the increased mastery by humans over environmental factors by means of improved technology, the very physiology of the processes of fertilization, incubation, and nurturance may change.

The possibility of fertilization and incubation apart from the individuals producing the gametes is becoming realizable. Patterns of nurturance are continuing to change, and it is evident that these will be drastically affected as fertilization and incubation procedures change. In the light of these changes the assignment of gender roles to an individual will also undergo significant changes. The relationship between behavioral patterns leading to reproduction and the physiology of reproduction will be redefined and altered.

Mastery of the technological aspects of environmental and physiological control of reproductive function will make it possible to bring the assignment of gender role under social control. The problem of human social behavior is to deal with the implications of these changes for the societal factors of gender assignment. Advanced technology has already changed the assignment of gender to particular occupations. The social process whereby the assignments and modifications of gender role take place will also require change, as at present these decisions usually take place without any planning, without necessary information, and frequently without regard for the equal rights of the individuals involved.

Changing social customs, traditions, and roles is inherent in being human. It seems invalid to attempt to use concepts from evolutionary biology to justify either retaining old traditions or changing them. The answer lies in understanding human history and behavior. Understanding the evolution of behavior, and in particular reproductive behavior, may help to clarify the problem, but cannot be the solution of contemporary problems in gender role assignment.

References

(1) HARLOW, H. 1963. The maternal affectional system. *In* Determination of Infant Behavior, II, B. Foss, ed. Methuen, London.

(2) SCHNEIRLA, T. 1957. Theoretical considerations of cyclic processes in doryline ants. Proc. Amer. Phil. Soc. 101: 106-113.

(3) SCHNEIRLA, T. 1957. The concept of development in comparative psychology. *In* The Concept of Development, D. Harris, ed. University of Minnesota Press, Minneapolis.

(4) SCHNEIRLA, T. 1966. Behavioral development in comparative psychology. Quart. Rev. Biol. 41:283—302.

(5) TAKAO, N., SHIMODA, C. and YANAGISHIMA, N. 1970. Chemical nature of yeast sexual hormones. Development, Growth and Differentiation 12:199—205.

(6) TOBACH, E. and SCHNEIRLA, T. 1968. The biopsychology of social behavior in animals. *In* The Biological Basis of Pediatric Practice, R. Cooke, ed. McGraw-Hill, New York.

CHANGING THE ROLE
OF WOMEN

Mordeca Jane Pollock

Women's liberation, or the New Feminism, is the second wave of an American social movement with intellectual roots reaching back at least to the eighteenth century, and political beginnings that may be traced to the nineteenth. While Mary Wollstonecroft's *Vindication of the Rights of Women* (1792) may be considered the first manifesto of conscious political feminism, the expression of feminism in literature and thought is clearly discernible from the troubadours through Virginia Woolf. In the nineteenth century, women in the temperance and abolition movements began to turn their eyes on their own status as women, as Eleanor Flexner has written in an impressively documented, if at times partisan, account of the first movement. To the temperance workers, it soon became obvious that without basic legal protections — in most states, woman had no legal recourse should her husband fail to support the family — their fight against social evil would never be won from the major opponent, the alcohol industry. The abolitionists began to compare their own legal servitude with the involuntary servitude of black slaves: Women's property was no longer their own once they married; women could not make contracts or engage in business on their own; any monies earned became their husbands'; and women did not have the franchise. Finally, the struggle to organize the American labor force included the struggle to end the exploitation of female labor in the mills and sweatshops of the industrial states.

The accomplishments of the "first movement," as it is called, are by no means inconsiderable. Starting with no political leverage, no money, and the overwhelming weight of conventional morality against them, the suffragists won those civil rights women now enjoy. Among their victories were the enactment of the Married Women's Property Acts in the latter half of the nineteenth century and, of course, the adoption of the Nineteenth Amendment to the Constitution in 1920. However, as historian Ann Firor Scott(13) notes:

> Until quite recently, American historians by and large have behaved as if women did not exist. In some major textbooks the whole history of American women takes up less space than a minor political party.(p. 1)

The period of prosperity and social change of the 1920s saw great advances in the social and economic status of women. But with the Depression and the war, gains women had made in many spheres were halted; indeed, a backward trend set in. After World War II, moreover, by dint of causes ranging from prosperity to prevailing psychiatric theory, American women fell under the influence of the *feminine mystique*. As redefined by Betty Friedan(4) and currently understood by American feminists, the term denotes the congruence of attitudes and values that defines a woman solely as a function of someone else (her husband and children) or some*thing* else (her homemaking activities). Consider the attributes valued most highly in American culture (individual striving, professional or political ambition, financial success) and those we have come increasingly to value (creativity, commitment to larger issues, self-realization). All were deemed abnormalities in women. Popular culture and accepted norms of "health" circumscribed women's activities and strivings; the image of the happy housewife shaped the lives and expectations of a whole generation of American women. As Friedan(4) wrote, there has grown up a whole generation of American women,

> who adjust to the feminine mystique, who expect to live through their husbands and children, who want only to be loved and secure, to be accepted by others, who never make a commitment of their own to society. . . . The adjusted or

cured ones who live without conflict or anxiety in the confined world of the home have forfeited their own being.(p. 300)

But the mystique was bound to lose its grip over women — for some very concrete reasons. From 1948 to 1970, the number of women in the American work force grew from 17.3 million to 31.1 million, so that women now constitute about 40% of those gainfully employed(14). Roughly 60% of the women who work *must* work: they are widowed, divorced, single, or their husbands earn less than $5,000 a year. Today there are about 18 million married women in the work force, and more than half of these women have children under eighteen years of age. Finally, one out of ten American families is headed by a woman.

Prosperity and technological sophistication, as well as changing economic patterns, have worked a revolution in women's life-styles. The burden of domestic labor has been potentially halved in the past fifty years. The increasing mobility dictated by economic circumstance has meant the virtual end of the extended family as the prevailing basic unit of American society and the emergence of the nuclear family. Increasing numbers of middle-class Americans have chosen to live in the "bedroom communities" of suburbia. As a result, women are often isolated from their men for half of the day and have, moreover, to confront hitherto unknown problems of childrearing and social interaction.

Advances in medical science and technology along with advances in our standard of living have created three profoundly revolutionary changes in women's life patterns: 1) We may now regulate the number of children to whom we give birth; 2) for the first time in human history, we may bring a limited number of children into the world with the reasonable assurance that they will live to maturity; and 3) we are the first generation of women in history to have a life-expectancy of three-quarters of a century — thirty years beyond the childrearing age.

In these changing circumstances, at least two eloquent voices rose to reawaken the feminist consciousness. In 1949, Simone de Beauvoir(2) analysed the attitudes that have cast women into the role of "the other," not really the full person. "To pose woman is to pose the absolute Other," she wrote, "without reciprocity, denying against all experience that she is a subject, a fellow human being." And in 1963, Friedan(4) discerned the cultural attitudes that had created a surprising *malaise* among American women: feelings of isolation and depression, a dimly perceived sense of worthlessness, emptiness, and frustration. The problems de Beauvoir and Friedan underscored frightened many women, for the implications of these problems are far-reaching indeed. At the same time, many women began to understand that feelings and situations they had thought to be personal were symptoms of a deeper, cultural illness that they had been conditioned to perceive as inevitable and natural.

The New Feminism is also an outgrowth of the new trends in political attitudes and participation that are the mark of the 1960s in the United States. Here, the experience of modern American feminists parallels that of their great-grandmothers in the suffragist movement. Working for civil rights, working for peace, working to elect male political candidates to high office — raising the funds, addressing the envelopes, pouring the coffee, but rarely participating in making the decisions — women turned their eyes to their own status. This shift in consciousness held equally true for SDS "chicks" and Republican committeewomen in the '60s as the nation underwent a revolution of rising political expectations.

It was therefore inevitable that women begin to examine their own status, the roles into which they had been cast, and their self-perceptions. Scrutinizing the economic sphere, women found that, in 1968, the average full-time female worker earned fifty-eight cents for every dollar the average full-time male worker earned. The median annual income for full-time work in that year was as follows: white males, $7800; non-white males, $5500; white females, $4500; non-white females, $3500. A female with four years of college earned on the average the same amount as a male with an eighth-grade education.(12) In 1970, of the 5.4 million American families headed by women, one out of every four was living below what the United States government deems the poverty level, while of the non-white families headed by women, one out of every two lived below the imaginary cut-off point.(6)

An analysis of jobs revealed that women are not only the victims of salary discrimination, but of type-casting in employment. Women are clerical, domestic, and sales "help," rather than industrial workers, crafts*men*, or managers.(12) Non-professional female workers do the housekeeping of business and industry and provide a supply of cheap labor. Women in the professions are conspicuous by their rarity, accounting for 1% of the nation's engineers, 7% of its physicians (the same proportion as in Spain), 9% of its scientists, 19% of its college and university professors. There are not even token numbers of women in the top jobs of business and industry.

Public and private educational institutions perpetuate women's economic disabilities. Members of the Boston Commission on the Status of Women recently found that vocational training programs in the high schools channel women into lower-paying jobs, while offering numerous courses for men in lucrative trades or skills. Three of the four college preparatory high schools in Boston do not admit women. In some states, women need higher grades than men to enter public colleges and universities. For example, "21,000 women were turned down for college entrance in the State of Virginia; during the same period not one application of a male was rejected."(16) Women have been virtually locked out of postgraduate education for the liberal professions. Harvard University, a quarter of whose undergraduates are female, did not admit women in its law school until after World War II; in March 1970, there were only 122 women in a total enrollment of 1,550 at Harvard Law School, according to the Registrar of the University. Education in the United States is far from coeducational; schools and universities reinforce women's vocational roles and allow the potential talents of half the population to remain untapped.

Despite the impressive achievements of the first movement, women are still inferior to men in the eyes of the law.(8) Social Security regulations actually penalize families with working wives.(11) While businessmen and professionals may deduct the most lavish expenses, working mothers usually may not deduct child care fees from their taxable income. The 1964 Civil Rights Act, which prohibits sex discrimination in employment, does not guarantee women's right to equity in education or public accommodations. In many states, a married woman does not have the right to choose her domicile, the address from which she votes, runs for office, attends the public schools or universities, or receives welfare assistance. Progress in upgrading women's legal status has been piecemeal because there is no clear constitutional guarantee of legal equality for women. And until very recently, the Federal courts, presided over almost exclusively by male judges, have not been willing to overturn discriminatory precedents. See Kanowitz,(8) pp. 149-196.

New Feminists examining the social legislation affecting women found that in areas such as paid maternity leave and job security for pregnant women, the United States lags dramatically behind other industrial countries. The nation is also remarkably retrograde in the area of child care facilities. In April 1970, it was reported to the President that 700,000 migrant children and 1,373,000 economically deprived children were in need of day care, a need singled out as "the most serious barrier to job training and employment for low income mothers."(11) These findings did not extend to all working mothers, yet we know that about nine million women in the work force have children under eighteen. Adequate parent-controlled facilities where children learn and grow are exceptional and, generally speaking, open only to the very affluent and some of the very poor. Most working women must be satisfied with inadequate child care facilities, or none at all.

Laws governing the termination of pregnancy through abortion have drawn both critical scrutiny and profound concern from feminists. In most states, it is virtually impossible — unless one is affluent, infirm, or mentally ill — to obtain an abortion under therapeutic conditions. Nonetheless, it has been estimated (the statistics are conservative) that at least a million American women undergo abortions every year.(9) Since the overwhelming majority of these operations are performed extra-legally, often under dangerous conditions, it comes as no surprise that at least a thousand women die each year at the hands of charlatans or due to their own efforts to induce abortion, and that eight out of ten of these women are non-white.(9)

Feminists believe that the criminal abortion statutes enforce involuntary servitude on women by determining how they are to use their bodies and spend their lives. It is cruel and unusual punishment to force a person to choose between breaking the law and risking sterilization or death on the one hand, and bearing an unwanted child on the other. But the issue of abortion has still other implications. The laws enforce a double standard of morality, punishing the woman for her sexual behavior while absolving the man involved. Beyond the issue of patriarchal sexual attitudes is the no less important issue of self-determination for women. To seek new life-styles and to make new life choices, women must exercise the basic right to control their own reproductive processes.

Examining women's political status, feminists have concluded that — the franchise notwithstanding — women's political power is non-existent. Although women constitute more than half of the nation's electorate, there are no women in high executive offices and not even token numbers in the legislative and judicial branches. Women are also absent from the powerful positions in business, industry, the military, and the universities, all of which influence, indeed may shape, political decision. Many feminists point to this lack of representation as dangerous, feeling that men's current conditioning tends to separate them from a full grasp of the worth of human life. Men have been trained to equate power with power *over* others, to view aggression as a valid means of problem-solving, and have thus become capable of dealing with the complicated mathematics of overkill while unable to confront the simple arithmetic of underfeed.

But these observable signs of women's status give only a partial picture of the limited life-style open to women who wish, or are conditioned, to follow the conventional path. A woman is expected to enter into a monogamous marriage, live in a nuclear – often emotionally isolated – family, and limit her activities to domestic concerns, volunteer work, and social interests that are, in the final analysis, severely circumscribed. A woman who chooses or is compelled to work is nonetheless expected to run the household and bear the major responsibility for child-rearing; she must make adjustments to marriage never asked of a man. The woman who chooses not to marry moves outside the mainstream of currently acceptable life-styles, and her penalty is often high. While men are also limited in their life patterns – monogamy and the nuclear family being the norm – they nonetheless enjoy a much wider choice of careers and social activities, and a greater potential influence on their community. Thus, women have been forced to make what have been called "half-choices." This applies as well to the type of interaction and self-perceptions expected of women. The taboos attendant upon types of interaction with men and, to a certain extent, with other women, are very restrictive. Women are conditioned to behave passively, whatever their emotions. Consider the meaning of the word "assertive" as applied to women and as applied to men.

All these aspects of women's role in society – her economic and legal disabilities, and restricted life-style – are signs of a psychologically enforced cultural myth, a set of assumptions and values concerning women that has been transmitted consciously and unconsciously for millennia.

Our very habits of speech reveal and perpetuate these values. *Roget's Thesaurus* lists the word "masculine" under the heading, "Strength," in a list of adjectives that includes, "strong, mighty, vigorous, stout, robust, irresistible, invincible, all-powerful." The adjective "womanish" is listed under the general heading of "Weakness," while synonyms for "effeminate" – often an insult in our language – are to be found under the headings, "Weak, womanlike, timorous, sensual." It is obvious that women are assumed to be less strong, less upright, less brave than men, for "manliness" is taken to denote desirable moral attributes.

Our religions consecrate and transmit the mythology revealed in our language. The young child who is taken to church hears the male minister speak of God as "He," "Our Father," "Lord our God, King of the Universe." Further, the puritanism characteristic of Western religions has projected onto women the feelings of guilt and sin erroneously and doggedly attached to sexuality. Indeed, the patristic writings are redolent with pathological anti-feminism.

Psychiatrists and psychologists – to whom we have looked increasingly for moral guidance – have also perpetuated the mythology; many have transmuted women's situation into her nature or essence. Thus, even the great Freud(5) could write that "women soon come into opposition to civilization and display their retarding influence. . . . The work of civilization has become increasingly the business of men, it confronts them with ever more difficult instinctual sublimations of which women are little capable." Following uncritically the lead of Freud, practitioners have been all too eager to qualify as "abnormal" females who do not wish to cast their identity in terms of their "primal instincts of sex and reproduction." Puritanism, and its placement of women in a lesser status, has entered through the back door. Hopelessly fudged accounts of women's psychological development and of female sexuality – mainly the result of implicit Victorianism and male fantasy – have also contributed to perpetuating the myths.

Consider the concept of "penis envy," which describes a political rather than a psychological reality. Here is Ernest Jones(7) on that topic: "What in the meantime has been the attitude toward the penis? It is likely enough that the initial one is purely positive, manifested by the desire to suck it. But penis envy soon sets in and apparently always." Pre-Masters and Johnson accounts of female sexuality are no less exaggerated in their error: "What man and woman, driven by obscure primitive urges, wish to feel in the sexual act, is the essential force of *maleness,* which expresses itself in a sort of violent and absolute *possession* of the woman." The same author(15) fared no better – and showed remarkable lack of neurological knowledge – when he wrote of female orgasm, "The final reflex in the woman may receive its signal from her realization of the muscular contractions of the man's orgasm; or from the impact of the vital fluid."

These linguistic habits and normative views rest on the assumption that females are by nature radically different from and, more important, inferior to men. The degree to which this sexism shapes the viewpoint even of counseling professionals, male and female, was suggested by a recent study(1) that found "behavioral attributes which are regarded as healthy for an adult, sex unspecified, and thus presumably viewed from an ideal, absolute standpoint, will more often be considered by clinicians as more healthy or appropriate for men than for women." While the authors impute this "double standard of health" to the adjustment viewpoint that they believe dominates counseling, I believe that the underlying "negative assessment of women" demonstrates the degree to which sexism molds even the most rationally based disciplines. It is a powerful mythology indeed that impels clinicians of both sexes to expect women *not* to react, think, and behave as adult persons.

The fantasy purveyors in advertising understand the potential of the myth, and manipulate it in its least rational manifestations. In their work, our norms of health, our God-given truths are metamorphised into a stream of injunctions. Women are told repeatedly that they will be valueless, lonely, unhappy unless they emulate the slim, glamourous, young model in the ads; they are told that, like the dumb housewife of another kind of ad, they will find security, fulfillment, even ecstasy in sinks and sheets that are whiter than white. Advertisements geared to men, tacitly or overtly promise adoring and available women as the reward for purchase.

If sexism is unjust and unrelated to reality, we must face the question, *Why the mythology?* Why are women defined as less than fully human, inferior in social interaction or civilization, capable only of circumscribed feeling and thinking, closer by nature to those functions and emotions we have cloaked in taboos — and, therefore, sinful?

The sexist mythology exists because the relationship between male and female is a political one, a relationship of superordinate to subordinate — and a relationship that obtains in the most intimate and personal as well as the most massive and public of our activities. This is, *grosso modo*, Kate Millet's(10) thesis in *Sexual Politics*. Once we deny any "natural" social and political inequality between men and women, the purpose of sexist propaganda becomes clear: to sanctify a situation that is by definition unfair, and that requires *ipso facto* the introjection by both parties of the values and conceptions necessary to maintain it.

Feminism, then, is a radical insight, intellectual and intuitive in its scope, that alone accounts for numerous phenomena — psychological, political, behavioral, and social.(6)

By the close of the last decade, many women who had become aware of the intellectual itinerary — and reached the conclusions — just outlined, set about to complete the unfinished business of their suffragist great-grandmothers.

Moderate feminists, who tend to construe women's liberation as a civil rights issue, see the unfinished business as that of equality. Groups such as the National Organization for Women have taken the initiative in pressing for long overdue equality of opportunity for women in employment and education. They are working for the enactment of social legislation to meet the needs of the 30 million women in the work force, for the funding and establishment of adequate child-care facilities, and for the winning of women's basic right to control what happens to and within their own bodies. Participation in current political life is central to the program of the moderates, who feel that only when women have substantial political power can their goals be achieved. For many moderates, women's participation in government would mean a massive realignment of national and international priorities. They believe that patriarchy has brought us to the doors of total war, eco-catastrophe, and overpopulation, and that it is time for women to wield the instrumentalities of power.

For radical feminists (a grouping that must be loosely defined, since varying ideologies interlock with radical feminism), the unfinished business of the first movement is the dissolution of patriarchy — its social and political forms, and the psychological attitudes and modes of thought it generates. To gain power within existing economic or political structures, they argue, is in itself a meaningless goal, since it is the institutions of patriarchy — from the "child-owning" nuclear family to the capitalist organizations that profit from sexism — that must be replaced. They see patriarchy, with its built-in forms of unjust dominance of others, at the root of most unwarranted uses and conceptions of power; since patriarchy is the prototype for existing forms of social organization and psychological conditioning, the programs of feminism must be revolutionary in character and shape. It is on this basis that radical feminists view women's liberation as "the ultimate revolution."

My own belief is that patriarchy has left us with no choice but to dissolve it; it is unjust and dangerous. We must replace it with more humane means of classifying human beings, and with more humane forms of social organization. The necessary first step is to render the sexist mythology inoperative by changing women's status now, and by altering women's ways of viewing themselves. It is this process that will engage the coming generation of women's liberationists; it is out of this process that the new conceptions of women, the new forms of human organization and interaction will develop.

References

(1) BROVERMAN ET AL. 1970. Sex role stereotypes and clinical judgments of mental health. J. Cons. Clin. Psychol. 34(1).

(2) DE BEAUVOIR, S. 1953. The Second Sex. Knopf, New York.

(3) FLEXNER, E. 1968. Century of Struggle. Atheneum, New York.

(4) FRIEDAN, B. 1964. The Feminine Mystique. Dell, New York.

(5) FREUD, S. 1961. Civilization and Its Discontents. Norton, New York.

(6) GORNICK, V. 1970. The light of liberation can be blinding. Village Voice (Dec. 10).

(7) JONES, E. 1966. The early development of female sexuality. *In* Psychoanalysis and Female Sexuality, H. Ruitenbeek, ed. College and University Press, New Haven.

(8) KANOWITZ, L. 1969. Women and the Law: The Unfinished Revolution. University of New Mexico Press, Albuquerque.

(9) LADER, L. 1966. Abortion. Beacon Press, Boston.

(10) MILLET, K. 1970. Sexual Politics. Doubleday, New York.

(11) PRESIDENT'S TASK FORCE ON WOMEN'S RIGHTS AND RESPONSIBILITIES. 1970. A Matter of Simple Justice: Message to Congress Proposing Legislation, April 1970, pp. 4-13.

(12) Rebelling women: the reason. U.S. News and World Report, April 13, 1970.

(13) SCOTT, A. 1970. Where we have been and where we are going. *In* What is Happening to American Women, A. Scott, ed. Southern Newspaper Publishers Association, Atlanta.

(14) U.S. DEPT. OF LABOR, WAGE AND LABOR STANDARDS ADMINISTRATION, 1970. Background Facts on Women Workers in the United States. U.S. Government Printing Office, Washington, D.C.

(15) VAN DE VELDE, T. 1959. Ideal Marriage: Its Physiology and Technique. Random House, New York.

(16) VIRGINIA COMMISSION FOR THE STUDY OF EDUCATIONAL FACILITIES IN THE STATE OF VIRGINIA, 1964.

THE IMPACT OF
THE WOMEN'S LIBERATION MOVEMENT
ON CHILD DEVELOPMENT BOOKS

Zelda S. Klapper

> *The important thing*
> *is to pull yourself up by your own hair*
> *to turn yourself inside out*
> *and see the whole world with fresh eyes*
> — Peter Weiss(72)

Regardless of the nature of its origins and independent of its destiny, the women's liberation movement has released a cascade of challenges at some of our most cherished notions in child development. One has only to scan one of their monthly schedules of seminars and workshops to appreciate the source of a growing body of new doctrine and dissent: "A Woman's Place – the Changing Image;" "The Nuclear Family;" "New Approaches to Child Rearing;" "Towards a New Feminism: Social and Political Aspects" (May, 1971 Newsletter, Westchester Women's Liberation Coalition).

There are five identifiable women's liberation movement propositions that are specifically relevant to the field of child care: 1) the nuclear family is an arbitrary development that may obstruct a child's optimum development; 2) early growth processes are not critically dependent upon the biological mother; 3) traditional gender-roles are artifically imposed upon children by the culture; 4) the assumption of gender-roles by children is counter-productive to their developmental health; and 5) mental health may be better ensured by the early transfer of responsibility for child rearing from the mother to the community.

Public attention has not been directed toward these five issues solely by the writings and speeches of members of the women's liberation movement. Various research and action projects have been initiated to monitor television commercials and stores in order to discourage the production of stereotyped gender-based toys such as fashion dolls and homemaking sets, pink for girls and blue for boys, etc.; a list has been compiled of children's "non-sexist" books by a collective of mothers, high school students, librarians, editors, and other professionals; collectively run infant-care centers have been established; male homosexual couples have petitioned to adopt children; the Erie County Family Court has approved the adoption of an eight-year-old girl by an unmarried, unrelated school-teacher.

But what about the books and texts in the field of child care and development? These provide an authoritative source of information for nonprofessionals as well as for child care specialists. To what extent are the authors and editors responding to the five women's liberation movement propositions?

The Effect of the Nuclear Family on Child Rearing Patterns

It is the women's liberation movement position that "the heart of woman's oppression is her child bearing and child rearing roles . . . the power hierarchies in the biological family, and the sexual repressions necessary to maintain it — especially intense in the patriarchal nuclear family — are destructive and costly to the individual psyche."(29) Further, the purpose of replacing the nuclear family with the extended or "organic" family is "to release the children from the disadvantages of being extensions of their parents so that they can belong primarily to themselves."(36) The core of women's distress is attributed by a psychiatrist(36) to the change from the dyadic family — mother and child — to the nuclear family.

In the texts reviewed, aside from an occasional speculative thought that it may not be necessary to have both father and mother to rear children,(25) the traditional view is preponderantly upheld:

> The child properly requires two parents: a parent of the same sex with whom to identify and who provides a model

to follow into adulthood, and a parent of the opposite sex
who becomes a love object and whose love and approval the
child seeks in return by identifying with the parent of the
same sex.(50)

Some would keep the family, but strongly recommend that a pet be
added to the core group.(45) Even more direct support is given to the
function of the nuclear family by those texts concerned with psychopathology and therapy in childhood with the thesis that "the child's
basic attachment is to his parents and ... no one can really replace
them,"(28) and that the "parent-child relationship [represents the]
most important single category of variables impinging on the personality development and socialization of the child."(7)

In no scholarly text is the view that parenthood is "a viciously
competitive sport, ostensibly for the sake of children"(44) brought up.
But neither is serious consideration given to Margaret Mead's well
known prediction that the family and marriage patterns as they now
exist will and should disappear by the year 2000. Professional journals,
periodicals, and newspapers cite her criticisms of the nuclear family and
its tradition of exclusive upbringing of a child by a close inseparable
mother with the negative consequence, among others, of the fear of
stranger and strangeness in the modern child. The reviewed books and
texts tend to disregard the existence of this point of view. What does
appear is concern for the strains imposed by the isolated nuclear family,
particularly in middle-class families deprived of institutionalized substi-
tutes for extended kin,(39) and the possibility that marriage is a
condition of risk for many women: one group of women identified as
the freest of mental illness was made up of middle-aged, unmarried
women who have careers.(64)

In an examination of family variation and mental health(5) the
depiction of some rather disastrous consequences in Senegal of the
transition from communal to nuclear family is presented without
reference to the possibly broader issues, although what is expressed
echoes women's liberation movement concern about the nuclear family:

> The family nucleus becomes the standard model. The father
> and the mother are the proprietors of the child as object,
> bearer of hopes and new values. ... The notion of plural
> "fathers and mothers" has no longer any connection with
> reality: the child no longer belongs to the group. He must

rapidly confront competition and solitude and be responsible for himself and his freedom. Relationship to the group has lost its strength and has been replaced by other narrower and more narcissistic investments: "to do" and "to have" fill the void left by the loss of being or personality.(19)

Although an occasional suggestion is made that it is a a myth that the middle-class nuclear family is the only possible kind of family, and that perhaps child rearing is too complex for the individual small family unit to deal with,(68) proposals of alternatives apparently evoke the same kind of dread of tampering with the forces of nature that has been captured in tales such as Howard Fast's,(27) in which "man-plus," the super child, is reared by placing children on 8,000 acres of national forest with thirty or forty parents to guide their growth. By the end of the tenth year, success was so complete and the children's cognitive growth so vast that teachers, parents, the outside world, and even spoken language were dispensed with.

It is in this context that the books reviewed consider such collective arrangements as the kibbutz, the age-mate camp, and the commune. Although Bronfenbrenner(14) has many positive thoughts about the USSR children's collective — with one upbringer for four children and peers for models — he questions the personal outcome. The Israeli kibbutz, in which children are brought up by professional *metapalets* or foster mothers, and with peer models, has also been questioned.(15, 57) Diffusely evaluated accounts of community-based group foster homes,(22) peer groups in general,(25,40) and one-parent homes(12) reflect some interest in the interactive processes, but, overall, the level of interest in the dynamics of peer interaction as a replacement for nuclear family models has been literary not scientific, grossly comparable to the science-fiction account of Fast.

The Biological Mother As Primary Upbringer

Betty Friedan has repeatedly claimed "It is the child who supports life in the mother . . . and he is virtually destroyed in the process." According to Edward Zigler's(76) recent statement as Director of the Federal Office of Child Development, "a fair mother is better than a good center."

Although current books acknowledge that in particular instances a particular mother may damage a child's psychological health,(2) not one author questions the availability of any evidence that the biological mother is, in fact, crucial in early development. The issue is simply not raised. Only indirectly, in studies of temperament differences in infancy,(17,18,66,70) is the traditional view that a child's early behavior directly and exclusively emerges from maternal practices challenged by research evidence. "Temperament must be given the same systematic attention that is now devoted to maternal and other environmental factors"(18) appears to be a cry in the wind.

Rather, the current books reviewed adhere closely to the traditional position that "the primary object relationship that ensures development [is] the child's need for the mother and the mother's readiness to fulfill this need."(6) Although some consider "the importance of mother's motivation for caretaking functions [and the] variations in the sensitivity of the mother to cues in the infant,"(38) for most, the liturgy is repeated that "motherly love is by its very nature unconditional ... nature, soil, the ocean."(30)

To the extent that serious consideration is currently given in these books to evidence related to the role of the mother in early life, the stress is likely to be equally placed on "the" mother and "mothering adults," and the nature of the infant's experience with the mothering adults,(9,41,57) with stress on the necessity of mothers loving their infants, and on "attachment." Research has been caught up with the entire question of early experiences and their positive effect on cognitive growth(2,74) The benefits of early stimulation are generally automatically tied in with the presence of the mother, even though there are no systematic studies of the importance of maternal attachment for healthy development. (In fact, there has been a suggestion(60) that "detachment" from the mother should be investigated as a class of behavior related to cognitive growth.) The tie-in prevails:

> The whole trend of recent work on the effects of separating the young child from his mother has been to show the vital importance for the individual's social development both of adequate stimulation during early infancy and also of the establishment during infancy of a stable relationship with a single mother-figure.(2)

The Origin of Gender Role in Children

According to Germaine Greer,(36) "The 'normal' sex roles that we learn to play from our infancy are no more natural than the antics of a transvestite."

In general, the current books in child development do address themselves to the issue of "masculine" and "feminine" behavior traits as products of socialization rather than the expression of innate sexual differences.(5,40,41,57) The presence of sex stereotypes in toys and books is acknowledged, and the processes of selective praise and punishment for sex differences in behavior and differential imitation of appropriate sex models are identified. "Children learn that girls play with dolls and boys with trains. They are not born with this information ... they are culturally conditioned."(4) However, the discussion of environmental influences on gender role is generally isolated from the recitative accounts of boy-girl differences in attitude, in temperament, in interests.(3) We read, for example, that "boys appear to cheat more than girls on what are regarded as 'masculine' tasks,"(41) etc.

There are also expressions of convictions that "Sex differences appear not because we expect them but we expect them because they emerge early,"(3) and that "genetic factors tend to be fundamental to the behavior patterns that emerge. Males are more active, aggressive, adventurous and object oriented. Females are more passive, accepting, nurturant and people-oriented."(65) In his recent book addressed to teen-agers, Spock(69) has proclaimed, "Biologically and temperamentally, I believe women are made to be concerned first and foremost with child care, husband care, and home care. Regretfully they have been 'confused' by their education." In most instances, these accounts merely imply what others have expressed, namely the belief that not only are these differences innate, but that they should be socially reinforced.

The Psychological Effect of Gender-Role Development

Independent of the issue of the origin of gender-role is the question of the psychological significance of developing an identity based largely upon gender-specific attitudes and behavior. The position of the women's liberation movement is centered on the deep concern about the lack of self-worth and the prevalent self-hatred that becomes part of the young girl's conscious and unconscious expectations of her future role and the process of being forced to accept an inferior role, learning to believe in her own inferiority. Although not as central, concern about the damaging effect on boys of gender-specific expectations, of having to be "manly," has been expressed by the women and by men who are sympathetic to the women's liberation movement.(26)

Aside from an occasional suggestion that "it may be that sex roles in terms of what is the masculine and what is the feminine thing to do are much less important than we thought them to be"(25) and that a more systematic study of sex differences in child rearing is needed,(5) no critical evaluation of gender role appears in the books reviewed. On the contrary, there are voiced complaints about the diffuseness of gender roles in primary reading textbooks, and neutral, non sex-linked male and female behavior,(57) expression of the need for fostering sex-role identity [as in Spock's cry that "mothers and fathers don't accentuate the differences in sex roles enough"(69)] and vigilance about a society that is about to rob the father of his power and status.(55)

Many traditional attitudes towards sex differences persist. Some texts(42) still provide growth charts of unclothed children with the sexual parts blocked out, and the eyes masked. Though the membership of NAMH has just adopted a position paper on homosexuality in which deviate sexual behavior is not regarded as a specific mental or emotional illness or as a danger either to individuals or to society, the treatment in current child development books of the issue of homosexuality is as it always was – disregarded. If mentioned, it is as if in passing, with one study(65) comparing pupillary reactions of heterosexual and homosexual men to pictures of nude women. Female homosexuality is never mentioned.

Transfer of Infant Rearing Responsibility to the Community

In Sweden, the women's liberation movement, Group 8, plans to include children from six months of age in day care centers. French law requires every community with a population of more then 2,000 to provide an *école maternelle* for children up to age six, and almost every community or urban center has its *creche* for infants as young as two months. In the creche, or infant nursery, trained baby nurses give infants their meals, fresh air and exercise, and are on duty from 7 a.m. to 7 p.m., including weekends and vacation periods.

In the face of claims from all over by infant-care-center advocates that the children do well, have less thumb-sucking, better verbal ability, and precocious coordination in these settings, there are no reports of, or projected designs for systematic studies of communal infant rearing. There is a widely expressed interest in the overall aspects of psychological development occurring before the child enters school, but as yet the fundamental issue of full-time infant care centers for women, across social class, is not being examined by child care specialists. What is indirectly expressed is resistance in the form of traditional assumptions, without evidence, that

> from the age of about 3 months to 3 years, ego growth is in the symbiotic phase; this is a critical period of development . . . anything that disrupts the mother-child relationship during this time will have a deleterious effect on the development of the youngster.(28)

Margaret Mead(51) comments in her recent review of Elizabeth Janeway's *Man's World, Woman's Place*, "the myth that woman's place is in the home . . . though patently untrue in many ways, forms the basis of most private attitudes and public discussions." And, one can add, of most of the books in the field of child care and development. This lack of responsiveness is possibly because the issues are too recent for current consideration, and probably because cultural attitudes are so firmly implanted. It is widely recognized that "the focus on childhood in American culture is unique. We have set a new record. No other people seems ever to have been so preoccupied with children, so anxious about them, or so uncertain of how to deal with them."(32)

It is distressing that the implications for child care and development that are part of women's reexamination and new consciousness of their lives and life styles have not been more directly confronted by those who are considered specialists in human development.

References

(1) ADLER, M. 1971. A Parent's Manual: Answers to Questions on Child Development and Child Rearing. Charles C. Thomas, Springfield, Ill.

(2) AMBROSE, A., ed. 1969. Stimulation in Early Infancy. Academic Press, New York.

(3) AMES, L. 1970. Child Care and Development. J. B. Lippincott, Philadelphia.

(4) ANSFIELD, J. 1971. The Adopted Child. Charles C. Thomas, Springfield, Ill.

(5) ANTHONY, E. and KOUPERNIK, C., eds. The Child In His Family Vol. I. Wiley-Interscience, New York.

(6) ANTHONY, E. and BENEDEK, T. 1970. Parenthood; Its Psychology and Psychopathology. Little, Brown, Boston.

(7) AUSBEL, D. and SULLIVAN, E. 1970. Theory and Problems of Child Development. Grune and Stratton; New York.

(8) BISCHOF, L. 1970. Interpreting Personality Theories. Harper & Row, New York.

(9) BOWLBY, J. 1969. Attachment and Loss. Vol. I, Attachment. Basic Books. New York.

(10) BOWLEY, A. 1970. Psychological assessment of young autistic children. *In* Non-Communicating Children, L. Minski and M. Shepperd, eds. Butterworths, London.

(11) BREASTED, M. 1970. Oh! Sex Education. Praeger, New York.

(12) BRECKENRIDGE, M. and MURPHY, M. 1969. Growth and Development of the Young Child. W. B. Saunders, Philadelphia.

(13) BRIGGS, D. 1970. Your Child's Self-Esteem: The Key to His Life. Doubleday, New York.

(14) BRONFENBRENNER, U. 1970. Two Worlds of Childhood. Russell Sage Foundation, New York.

(15) BUXBAUM, W. 1970. Troubled Children in a Troubled World. International Universities Press, New York.

(16) CALLAHAN, S. 1971. The Working Mother. Macmillan, New York.

(17) CHESS, S., THOMAS, A and BIRCH, H. 1965. Your Child is a Person. Viking Press, New York.

(18) CHESS, S. 1969. An Introduction to Child Psychiatry. Grune & Stratton, New York.

(19) COLLOMB, H. and VALANTIN, S. 1970. Family variation and mental health. *In* The Child in His Family Vol. I. E. Anthony and C. Koupernik, eds. Wiley-Interscience, New York.

(20) COOPER, D. 1971. The Death of the Family. Pantheon, New York.

(21) COTTLE, T. 1971. Time's Children: Impressions of Youth. Little, Brown, Boston.

(22) D'AMATO, G. 1970. Residential Treatment for Child Mental Health. Charles C. Thomas, Springfield, Ill.

(23) DITTMAN, L. 1970. Early Child Care: The New Perspectives.

(24) EYSENCK, H. 1970. The Structure of Human Personality. John Dickens, London.

(25) FAISON, R. et al. 1969. The Future of the Family. Family Service Association of America, New York.

(26) FARRELL, W. 1971. The Human Lib. Movement – I. New York Times, June 17.

(27) FAST, H. 1970. The first men. *In* The Worlds of Science Fiction. Paperback Library, New York.

(28) FINCH, S. and MC DERMOTT, R. 1970. Psychiatry for the Pediatrician. W. W. Norton, New York.

(29) FIRESTONE, S. 1970. The Dialectic of Sex. Bantam, New York.

(30) FROMM, E. 1956. The Art of Loving. Harper & Row, New York.

(31) GARDNER, G. 1970. The Emerging Personality: Infancy Through Adolescence. Delacorte, New York.

(32) GOODMAN, M. 1970. The Culture of Childhood. Teachers College Press, New York.

(33) GOODWIN, R. 1970. Where We Are: A Hard Look at Family and Society. Child Study Association, New York.

(34) GORDON, I. 1971. Baby Learning Through Baby Play: A Parent's Guide for the First Two Years. St. Martin's Press, New York.

(35) GORDON, T. 1970. Parent Effectiveness Training: The "No-Lose" Program For Raising Responsible Children. Wyden, New York.

(36) GREER, G. 1971. The Female Eunuch. McGraw-Hill, New York.

(37) GUILLAUME, P. 1971. Imitation of Children. University of Chicago Press.

(38) HAMBURG, D. 1969. In Stimulation in Infancy, A. Ambrose, ed. Academic Press, New York.

(39) HANKEL, G. 1970. Sociological Aspects of Parenthood. In Parenthood: Its Psychology and Psychopathology, E. J. Anthony and T. Benedek, eds. Little, Brown, Boston.

(40) HARTUP, W. 1970. Peer Interaction and Social Organization. In Manual of Child Psychology, P. H. Mussen, ed. Wiley, New York.

(41) HOFFMAN, M. 1970. Moral Development. In Carmichael's Manual of Child Psychology, Vol. II. Wiley, New York.

(42) HURLOCK, E. 1970. Child Growth and Development. McGraw-Hill, New York.

(43) JEFFERS, C. 1970. A New Look at Old Stereotypes of Family Life. Child Study Association, New York.

(44) LEAR, M. 1963. The Child Worshipers. Crown, New York.

(45) LEVINSON, B. 1969. Pet-Oriented Child Psychotherapy. Charles C. Thomas, Springfield, Ill.

(46) LINDGREN, H. and BYRNE, D. 1971. Psychology: An Introduction to a Behavioral Science. Wiley, New York.

(47) LOVE, H. 1970. Parental Attitudes Toward Exceptional Children. Charles C. Thomas, Springfield, Ill.

(48) LOVE, H. 1970. The Emotionally Disturbed Child: A Parent's Guide. Charles C Thomas, Springfield, Ill.

(49) LIDZ, T. 1967. Karen Horney Lecture, Association for the Advancement of Psychoanalysis, March.

(50) LIDZ, T. 1970. The Person. Basic Books; New York.

(51) MEAD, M. 1971. Sunday Times Book Review. June 20.

(52) MC CAMMON, R. 1970. Human Growth and Development. Charles C Thomas, Springfield, Ill.

(53) MC DOUGALL, J. and LEVOVICI, S. 1969. Dialogue with Sammy. Hogarth Press, London.

(54) MINSKI, L. and SHEPPERD, M. 1970. Psychiatry for the Pediatrician. Butterworths, London.

(55) MITSCHERLICH, A. 1970. Society Without the Father: A Contribution to Social Psychology. Schocken, New York.

(56) MORGAN, R. 1970. Sisterhood is Powerful. Vintage Books. Random House, New York.

(57) MUSSEN, P., CONGER, J. and KAGAN, J., eds. 1970. Readings in Child Development and Personality. Harper & Row, New York.

(58) MUSSEN, P., ed. 1970. Carmichael's Manual of Child Psychology. Wiley, New York.

(59) PICKARD, P. 1970. Psychology of Developing Children. Longman Group Ltd.

(60) RHEINGOLD, H. 1970. The infant separates himself from his mother. Science 168 (April):78-83.

(61) ROSENTHAL, R. 1971. Vast Plan for Health, Educational and Social Service to Children. Gains in Congress. N.Y. Times, June 14.

(62) RUBIN, I. and KIRKENDALL, L., eds. 1970. Sex in the Childhood Years: Expert Guidance for Parents, Counselors and Teachers. Association Press, New York.

(63) RUTTER, M., TIZARD, J., WHITMORE, K., eds. 1970. Education, Health, and Behavior. Longmans, Green, London.

(64) RUTTER, M. 1970. Sex differences in children's responses to family stress. *In* The Child in His Family. Vol. I. E. J. Anthony and C. Koupernik, eds. Wiley-Interscience, New York.

(65) SANFORD, F. and WRIGHTMAN, L., eds. 1971. Psychology: A Scientific Study of Man. Brooks/Cole.

(66) SHAFFER, H. and EMERSON, P. 1964. The Development of Social Attachments in Infancy. Monog. Society Research Child Development Ser no 94m vol. 29, #3.

(67) SHIFF, J. and SHIFF, B. 1971. All My Children. Lippincott.

(68) SINGER, P. 1970. Family for What? *In* Where We Are: A Hard Look at Family and Society. Child Study Association, New York.

(69) SPOCK, B. 1970. A Teenager's Guide to Life and Love. Simon and Schuster, New York.

(70) THOMAS, A., CHESS, S. and BIRCH, H. 1968. Temperament and Behavior Disorders in Children. New York University Press.

(71) THOMAS, W. and THOMAS, D. 1970. The Child in America. Alfred A. Knopf, New York.

(72) WEISS, P. 1966. Marat/Sade. Atheneum, New York.

(73) WERNER, H., ed. 1970. New Understanding of Human Behavior. Association Press, New York.

(74) WHITE, B. 1970. Child Development Research: An Edifice Without a Foundation. *In* Readings in Child Development and Personality. P. H. Mussen *et al.*, eds. Harper and Row, New York.

(75) WUNDERLICH, R. 1970. Kids, Brains and Learning: What Goes Wrong – Prevention and Treatment. Johnny Reads Publ.

(76) ZIGLER, E. 1971. New York Times, June 14.

THE ACCEPTANCE OF THE CONCEPT OF THE MATERNAL ROLE BY BEHAVIORAL SCIENTISTS: ITS EFFECTS ON WOMEN

> *"The maternal 'instinct' is a comfortable male myth; a woman can only give freely if she is in a position where she does not feel deprived herself."*
>
> — S. Gail(12)

The purpose of this review is to reexamine critically the importance of the concept of "mothering" and to suggest that much of the evidence employed in psychological studies of the importance of the mother for the development of infants and children is based on assumptions that are scientifically inadequate. Furthermore, modern psychology, with its emphasis on individual advancement, individual achievement, and individual development, has encouraged the isolation of the adult woman, particularly the mother, and the domestication and subordination of females in society.

I am here challenging a concept that has for generations been viewed as a biological and social necessity. It is important, however, to discuss some of the contradictions inherent in our system of child-rearing that have overwhelming negative, oppressive effects on half the population (women) and on all infants who develop in the environment of the nuclear family, with its prevailing emphasis on the mother-infant socialization process.

There are four basic questions to bear in mind when reading the literature on mother-infant interaction:

1) Is it a biological fact that, in the human species, the mother is the most capable person to socialize the infant?

2) Is it a biological fact that the human newborn seeks out the mother (rather than the father) or a female (rather than a male) as the figure to which it naturally relates best, needs most, and attaches itself to socially?

3) Socially, what criteria should we employ to define whether it is beneficial for the infant to form a strong bond of attachment to one woman?

4) Is it beneficial for the mother to assume the principal responsibility for the care and socialization of the young child?

We must begin with the understanding that we all have a strong prejudice about the need for "mothering" because we were all mothered. In a society such as ours, in which mothering is the principal mode of rearing children, any variant pattern that occurs (such as "multiple mothering," infants being raised by their fathers, or group rearing of infants) is considered abnormal. Participants in such variant patterns are constantly reminded of the "fact" that what they are doing is an exceptional alternative, a poor substitute for the "normal" pattern. This implies that they could never equal or improve upon the norm.

Margaret Mead has long been questioning the provincialism of studies of mother-infant interaction by Western psychologists and psychiatrists. In particular, Mead criticized the emphasis on the exclusive mother-infant bond. She emphasized that the conscious care of the infant is a cultural, not a biological one. According to Mead, diversified kinds of attachment relationships have been successful in other cultures.(24) In our society, on the other hand, the vast majority of women are conditioned to expect that the child-rearing function will be their major individual responsibility.

Attachment

The "Attachment Function," as defined and elaborated by John Bowlby,(7) is a dual process through which the infant develops a strong psychobiological need to maintain proximity with the mother while the mother has a strong psychobiological need to maintain proximity with the infant. Attachment behavior usually begins to appear at around four to six months and, during the first year of life, a strong affectional bond develops.(1,7) An "autonomous propensity" by the mother and infant to develop attachment toward each other is assumed by Bowlby's theory. This aspect of the theory will be discussed later in this paper.

The primacy of the mother-infant attachment is contradicted by Schaffer and Emerson's(35) study of attachment. They described three different stages in the development of attachment behavior: an "asocial" stage, in which the infant actively seeks optimal stimulation from *all* aspects of the environment; a "presocial" stage, in which the infant indiscriminately seeks proximity to objects that give it satisfaction; and, finally, a "social" stage, in which attachments to specific individuals occurs. Schaffer and Emerson concluded that:

> To focus one's enquiry on the child's relationship with the mother alone would therefore give a misleading impression of the attachment function. . . . In certain societies multiple object relationships are the norm from the first year on: the relevant stimuli which evoke attachment behavior are offered by a number of individuals and not exclusively one person, and a much more diversified system of attachments is thus fostered in the infant.(pp. 70-71)

That there is no evidence for the assumption that attachments must be confined to only one object, the mother, nor that all other attachments are subsidiary to the mother-infant bond, was one of the findings of their study. They concluded that:

> Whom an infant chooses as his attachment object and how many objects he selects depends, we believe, primarily on the nature of the social setting in which he is reared and not on some intrinsic characteristic of the attachment function itself."(p. 71)

Finally, Shaffer and Emerson suggested that while the mother tends to be present in the child's environment for most of the time, this does not guarantee that she will provide the quantity and quality of stimulation necessary for optimal development of the infant. A recent experimental-observational study by Kotelchuck,(20) one of the few studies on father-infant interaction, demonstrated that one-to-two year old infants are equally attached to their fathers and mothers. Furthermore, the strength of attachment to fathers correlated with the degree to which the fathers cared for their children during their development.

Separation

The principal argument used to encourage women to devote their constant attention to newborns is based on the suggested deleterious effects of mother-child separation. This is the "Bowlby-"(5) or "Spitz-hypothesis."(38,39) Most of the studies of mother-child separation have been based, however, not on normal separation of infants from their parents, but on institutionalized children. Because of the physical and social sterility of many hospitals and orphanages, these children often suffered from inadequate environmental and human stimulation.(10,44) The mother-child separation studies have not provided an adequate history of "the reasons which led to the children studied being uprooted from their homes or about the conditions in which they lived before this happened," according to Barbara Wootten.(43) She comments that:

> One can hardly assume that the boys and girls found in a Children's Home constitute a fair sample of the child population generally: something unusual either in themselves or their environment must have happened to account for their being deprived of ordinary family life.(p. 146)

Yarrow's(44) review of studies published between 1937 and 1955 concluded that most of the studies of institutionalized infants selected subjects who were already under treatment for emotional or personality disturbances. Furthermore, they were lacking in data on the early conditions of maternal care. In addition, Yarrow wrote,

> The dramatic character of these changes [i.e., reactions of infants to separation from the mother] has overshadowed the significant fact that a substantial portion of the children in each study did not show severe reactions to separation.(p. 474)

Casler(10) concluded that,

> none of the clinical or institutional studies ostensibly supporting the "Spitz-Ribble hypothesis" really does so, simply because none is able to demonstrate that probable

causes of the adverse effects of institutionalization, other than maternal deprivation, are inoperative.(p. 12)

Casler further described several studies in which institutionalized babies showed no ill effects. Pinneau, who published several articles(30, 31, 32) dissecting methodological inadequacies of the Spitz and Ribble studies, concluded(32) that

> It may well be that the burden of blame for the uncritical acceptance of his work does not rest with Spitz, who has published his results as he sees them, but rather with those who have acclaimed his work, and whose research training should enable them to make a critical evaluation of such research reports.(p. 462)

Positive alternatives to traumatic separation of infant and mother have not been sufficiently discussed in the psychological literature. In fact, there seems to have occurred a dangerously unscientific extrapolation of assumptions from studies of institutionalized infants to the much more common situation in which infants leave their homes for part of the day, are cared for by other responsible individuals, and are returned again to their homes. As a result, women are taught to believe that infants require their undivided attention during the first two or three years of life, at least. The way our society is structured, this attitude functions to confine the woman physically (to her home) and socially (to her family unit). Neil O'Connor(28) observed:

> There is some danger that by analysing one source of emotional disturbance, such as mother-child separation, the interaction of the society and the family may be neglected, and the family considered as if it were an isolated unit, which alone determines the behaviour of individuals in all their social relations.(p. 188)

On this matter, Margaret Mead wrote:

> At present, the specific biological situation of the continuing relationship of the child to its biological mother and its need for care by human beings are being hopelessly confused in the growing insistence that child and biological mother, or mother surrogate, must never be separated, that all separation, even for a few days is inevitably damaging,

and that if long enough it does irreversible damage. This . . . is a new and subtle form of antifeminism in which men — under the guise of exalting the importance of maternity — are typing women more tightly to their children than has been thought necessary since the invention of bottle feeding and baby carriages. Actually, anthropological evidence gives no support at present to the value of such an accentuation of the tie between mother and child. . . . On the contrary, cross-cultural studies suggest that adjustment is most facilitated if the child is cared for by many warm friendly people.(p. 477)

Finally, returning to the experience of natural separation between parents and children, none of the studies of children of working mothers has demonstrated systematic differences between children who are home all the time and children whose mothers work.(45,46) However, because the Bowlby-Spitz hypothesis has had such a profound impact on child-rearing practice, legislators, employers and educators have refused to provide sufficient adequate free childcare for working women.(46) Consequently, working women are usually forced to find their own, individual solutions to the child-care problem. Even in "dual-career" families (families in which the mother and father both have professional careers), the men and women tend to accept as inevitable that women should take on the major responsibility for the organization of child-care and the household in addition to their career responsibilities.(33) The consequence is that the women in such families carry the strain of both career and family problems. Apparently this is a major problem in Eastern European socialist countries as well as in Western society.(33,46)

The excellent reviews mentioned above, on the subject of separation and institutionalization, share in criticizing overgeneralizations that have been drawn from separation studies. Several reviewers (10,44) attempted to analyze the objective variables that the mothering function provides for the healthy growth and emotional security of the developing infant. However, none has sufficiently questioned the concept that the mother must be the one who does the mothering. Yudkin and Holme(46) wrote:

Most of the literature, however, tends to stress the value of the exclusive mother-child relationship and to ignore the possibility or even the need, for its dilution. This is to attempt to justify a particular, local and almost certainly, temporary, economic and cultural pattern as an eternal biological law. This can only do a disservice to both the mothers and the children.(p. 138)

Naturalism and Instinct Theory

The assumption that the biological mother must be the major responsible adult in the infant's life is intimately related to the theory that women have an instinct to mother. The assumption is based on observations, from the earliest recorded history, that confirm that women are usually the ones who nurture and raise children, specifically their own children. An entertaining and informative article by Una Stannard(40) attempts to document that "Women have the babies, but men have the maternal instinct." In her historical paper, Stannard reminds us that the major books and manuals telling women how to be good mothers have been written by men.

It remains an assumption, or hypothesis, however, that what we observe and describe naturalistically is what is biologically correct or socially optimal. John Stuart Mill, quoted in Millett(25), wrote:

the unnatural generally means only uncustomary, and . . . everything which is usual appears natural. The subjection of women to men being a universal custom, any departure from it quite naturally appears unnatural.(p. 94)

In the words of Eriksen, quoted in Casler(10),

While most of us will continue to believe in the importance of mothering during infancy, we must recognize that this belief has more the characteristics of a faith and less the basis of demonstrated fact.(p. 9)

Ethology, the study of animals in their natural environments, has had a strong influence on recent practice in human developmental psychology. Bowlby(6) has been one of the principal protagonists in the trend to return to naturalistic observations of human and animal behavior:

Until recent years, most of the knowledge available about mother-infant interaction in humans was either anecdotal or else a result of reconstructions based on data derived from older subjects. In the past decade, however, enquiries have been begun which have as their aim, the systematic descriptive and causal study of what actually occurs during a baby's interaction with the humans who care for him. (p. xiii)

However, ethologists, carrying out descriptive studies of behavior, have not approached their observational tasks bias-free. The discipline of ethology has long been linked with instinct theory, which attributes the organization of complex patterns of species-typical behavior to hypothetical, pre-formed biological models.(22,42) On the human level, instinct theory emphasizes the biological pre-destination of psychological characteristics. Branch(4) states:

The Freudian view of man's nature starts from the assumption that he is really a nonsocial or even an antisocial creature. His primary needs are not social but individual and biological. This means that society is not essential to man but is something outside his nature, an external force to whose distorting pressures he is victim.(p. 96)

Critics of instinct theory have stressed its neglect of the social and developmental history of the organisms being observed and its failure to view the organism as one that both affects and is affected by the biosocial environment in which it develops.(21,36) Bowlby's theory of attachment behavior(1,7) is an interactionist one. However, it assumes that there are certain features of the environment that the infant is biologically structured to be particularly sensitive to. The theory assumes that the environment of the newborn is optimal, and that the infant is biologically predisposed to adapt to it. As summarized by Ainsworth,(1)

ethologists hold that those aspects of the genetic code which regulate the development of attachment of infant to mother are adapted to an environment in which it is a well-nigh universal experience that it is the mother (rather than some biologically inappropriate object) who will be present under conditions which facilitate the infant's becoming attached to her.(pp. 995–996)

Such a theory is conservative because it neglects the enormous range of socio-cultural environments into which newborn infants are thrust and idealizes the mother-infant couple, which, as Orlansky(29) pointed out long ago, is "one conforming to an ideal-typical norm held by Western psychiatrists."(p. 15)

It is frequently argued that the human female, like other mammals, is biologically best equipped to respond to the needs of a newborn because of her long period of biological, hormonal and psychological priming during pregnancy. It has been suggested, for instance, that in the period immediately after birth, mothers may be particularly sensitive to the needs of their babies.(7) This may indeed be true. However, it is also true that a woman who has just had her first child, and who has not previously handled, fed, or cared for an infant, has great difficulty in the first days of the baby's life in establishing feeding, whether it be by breast or bottle. New mothers often have to be told how to hold the baby, burp it, bathe it, and dress it. Of course, most women learn how to care for their infants quite efficiently within a short period of time, through practice and determination.

Recent studies have demonstrated that infants play an active role, even in the first weeks of life, in getting their needs satisfied. There is now extensive literature on the way in which the infant actively initiates social interaction and is capable of modifying the behavior of the adult who cares for it.(3,41) This means that the infant helps the adult to develop appropriate responses that will bring about the satisfaction of its needs. This, in turn, means that, given a socially acceptable alternative, the mother need not be the principal caretaker of her own infant, although many women may still want to enjoy this responsibility.

Most evidence today indicates that the factors that are important for healthy infant and child development are: consistent care; sensitivity of the caretaking adult(s) in responding to the infant's needs; a stable environment, the characteristics of which the growing infant can learn to identify; continuity of experience within the infant's environment; and physical and intellectual stimulation, love, and affection. "There is no clear evidence," Yarrow(44) wrote, "that multiple mothering, without associated deprivation or stress, results in personality damage." And Mead(24) wrote,

> The problem remains of how to separate the necessary protection of a child who has been isolated in an exclusive pair relationship with the mother — of a type which cannot be said to be natural at a human level, because it actually

does not permit participation by the father, care of the
dependent older siblings, and ties with the three-generation
family, all of which are human experiences – from advo-
cacy of the artificial perpetuation or intensification or
creation of such conditions of exclusive mother-child dependence.(p. 58)

Unlike other reviewers,(17,27,46) who advocate reforms for women
that would alleviate the strains of dual or triple careers, while basically
accepting the assumption that only women can perform the mothering
function, I would like to emphasize that it is scientifically unacceptable
to advocate the natural superiority of women as child-rearers and
socializers of children when there have been so few studies of the
effects of male-infant or father-infant interaction on the subsequent
development of the child.

The acceptance of the concept of mothering by social scientists
reflects their own satisfaction with the status quo. The inability of
social scientists to explore or to advocate alternatives to current
child-rearing practices is due to their biased conception of what should
be studied and to their willingness to advocate social change. As Myrdal
and Klein(27) recognized,

the sentimental cult of domestic virtues is the cheapest
method at society's disposal of keeping women quiet
without seriously considering their grievances or improving
their position. It has been successfully used to this day, and
has helped to perpetuate some dilemmas of home-making
women by telling them, on the one hand that they are
devoted to the most sacred duty, while on the other hand
keeping them on a level of unpaid drudgery.(p. 145)

The time has come to evaluate more critically the ways in which the
home and the single mothering figure *fail* to provide the kind of
environment that is optimally stimulating or satisfying to the growing
infant.

Mother's Feelings and the Needs of Women

A young housewife(12) writes:

I feel it should be more widely recognized that it is in the
very nature of a mother's position, in our society, to avenge

her own frustrations on a small, helpless child; whether this
takes the form of tyranny, or of a smothering affection that
asks the child to be a substitute for all she has missed.
(p. 153)

It is important to recognize that many young mothers have ambiva-
lent feelings about the responsibility of motherhood. Hannah Gavron's(13) survey of women in London showed that

the majority of wives, both working-class and middle-class,
appear from the discussion of their own views on home and
work to be essentially on the horns of a dilemma. They
want to work, feel curiously functionless when not working, but at the same time they sense their great responsibilities towards the children. In both groups those who
were at home gave the children as their main reason for
being there.(p. 122)

My own experience, studying the development of feeding behavior in
infants, corroborates this. I studied mature, healthy, full-term babies,
all the products of normal pregnancies and deliveries. The mothers were
not tense or unhappy women with unusual medical or psychological
histories. Yet, many of the women expressed the same conflicts:
boredom, sense of isolation being home alone with the baby, desire to
be able to get back to work, and doubts about finding adequate
child-care facilities should they have the opportunity of getting employment. Most of the women, whether they wanted to work or not, had
the feeling that it would be wrong to go out to work because it might
somehow endanger the infant's well-being. The study of Yarrow and
her colleagues(45) demonstrated that, "Mothers who prefer to work
but out of a sense of 'duty' do not work report the most problems in
child rearing."(p. 122)

The negative effects of too intensive a relationship developing
between mother and child, leading to a clinical pattern of "overprotec-
tion," are discussed by Myrdal and Klein.(27) Herzog(17) gives passing
mention to the fact that "it is no secret that some mothers are not
loving, and some who are do not want to devote themselves exclusively
to infant or child care."(p. 18). A recent book(11) on child-rearing
restates the problem:

The role in which most contemporary theorists of child

development cast the mother makes it hard for her and hard for her children. What's more, the evidence indicates that she has been *mis*cast. No matter how seriously she takes the demand on her for omnipotence, and no matter how omnipotent the performance she turns out, there is no guarantee that the act will come off. All too often the child fails to reflect the best parents' most studious try for perfection.(p. 14)

We must now turn our attention to the home. We are taught that the best environment for the growth and development of a healthy child is provided within the individual home. The home environment, however, is socially sterile because mobility, outside stimulation, exchange of ideas and socially productive relationships are, as Myrdal and Klein(27) point out, severely limited there:

> The isolated woman at home may well be kept "in touch" with events, but she feels that the events are not in touch with her, that they happen without her participation. The wealth of information which is brought to her without any effort on her part does not lose its vicariousness. It increases rather than allays her sense of isolation and of being left out.(p. 148)

Yudkin and Holme(46) discuss the effects of the physical and social isolation of small families in which:

> a large number of children are tied almost exclusively to their mothers for the first five years of life, having little opportunity to meet any other people or to develop the beginnings of social relationships, let alone to explore the world outside their own home, until the sudden and dramatic beginning of their school life. Such isolation is obviously likely to increase the closeness and intensity of the relationship between the mother and her young children and may well have an effect on the type of adult personality that results, but whether the effect is good or bad is another matter.(pp. 137–138)

An English housewife(12) wrote:

> Housework is housework, whoever does it. It is a waste socially, psychologically, and even economically, to put me in a position where my only means of expressing loyalty to

[the baby] is by shopping, dish-washing and sweeping floors. I have trained for teaching literature to university students; it would be far more satisfying to guide a nursery class with Carl in it than it is to feel too harassed by irrelevant jobs to pay his development much attention. (p. 148)

The home, therefore, is physically restrictive and, for many women, is felt to be socially restrictive as well. In the home, one's economic and personal tensions and problems are most pronounced. These factors have a profound effect on the mother and child confined to the home, and are a principal influence on the physical, intellectual, and social development of children coming from different social class backgrounds. Bruner's(8) recent review of studies dealing with the cognitive development of children from different social class backgrounds, is rich in examples of the complex way in which feelings of powerlessness by the mother are conveyed to the children and affect the children's ability to cope with their environment.

Current studies of mother-child interaction in the United States, comparing children of working-class mothers with children of middle-class mothers, have ostensibly demonstrated the "cognitive superiority" of the latter. The conclusions of such research are that working-class mothers have to be taught to behave like middle-class mothers. The form of implementation recently adopted to help these women and their children, is to teach working class women how to provide optimal maternal stimulation to the child within the home environment. However, no programs are implemented to provide working-class women with the advantages of class privilege that middle-class women enjoy, since it is beyond the power of the behavioral scientist to effect such changes in the social and economic status of the people concerned [*How Harvard Rules Women*,(18) pp. 66–74]. Hunt's(19) recommendation that parent-child centers become the focus of intervention programs by professionals to teach "competence" to poverty mothers and their children was aptly criticized by Gordon,(15) who wrote:

Hunt is proposing a strategy that, like most formal education, essentially seeks to upgrade black and poor people by identifying all those things that are "wrong" with them, and changing those things. Such a strategy, with its implied criticism and its prescription for the adoption of goals and values of the oppressors, should hardly be imposed upon a

group by outsiders, no matter how well intentioned. More
effective programs of assistance are likely to come from
among the people themselves.(p. 41)

One might add that the people, in this case working-class mothers,
might feel that other individuals should be involved in the process of
child-rearing and that the responsibility for the socialization of children
should not rest on the mothers alone.

In the past and present, day-care programs for children have been
officially encouraged during periods of economic strain, when women's
labor was necessary for production. Neither economics nor women's
needs to get out of the home, however, are sufficient justification for
child-care centers. Good day-care programs are a necessity for infants
and children because they encourage the development of cooperative
social interaction during a period of life in which, in modern Western
society, children receive insufficient experience with other trusting,
loving, dependable children and adults. In the words(16) of two
day-care workers:

> It is well documented that attitudes toward work, race, sex
> (including male/female roles), initiative, and cooperation
> are formed during the first five years of life. It follows that
> we need to be seriously concerned with what happens
> inside the day care center.
>
> What goes on between the child and the environment
> (whether it's a home or a day-care center) affects the kind
> of capacities that the child will have as an adult. The ability
> to feel deeply and be sensitive toward other people, the
> ability to trust oneself and use one's initiative, the ability to
> solve problems in a creative and collective way — these all
> can be given their foundation or stifled in the first five
> years.
>
> By the age of 4 children are taking in the idea that a
> woman's place is in the home. Three and four year old
> children are already learning that it's better to be white.
> They are learning to follow directions and rules without
> asking why. They are learning how to deny their own
> feelings and needs in order to win approval from adults.
>
> These are examples of learning that most commonly
> result from early childhood experiences. These are elements
> of the invisible curriculum that usually forms the child's
> environment in our society.(pp. 27–28)

Recognizing the social needs of mothers and infants, some investigators have begun to encourage entry into day nurseries at much earlier ages than is customary. While these efforts were, at first, strongly criticized by workers in the field, the findings were very encouraging: assessments made at thirty months showed that children from lower-class families who were enrolled in a day-care center from about one year of age did not differ from home-reared children in the strength of attachment to their mothers. Likewise, mothers of day-care infants did not show any differences from home-mothers in intensity of attachment to their infants. The study(9) showed that, while the home-reared group declined in developmental quotient at thirty months, the day-care infants increased in developmental level.

I am convinced that new studies will continue to demonstrate that stable, loving, stimulating group environments can produce healthy, affectionate, bright youngsters, and that, quite early in life, infants can spend a good part of their day away from their homes and parents without adverse consequences. The problem ahead of us is to analyze the relationship between the nuclear family and the functioning of society, and to study and create the conditions under which the home ceases to confine the woman and the child to social and productive isolation. The fact is that, in modern Western society, no other institutions offer the adult the comfort, the emotional security, the loyalty, and the emotional dependability that the modern family provides. Even saying this, it is necessary to recognize the converse, that for many children and women, the modern family is a prison, breeding repression, unequal relationships and authoritarian conformity. The evolution of the family and its relationship to societal structure has been the basis for a good deal of study and renewed analysis.(14,26, 34) I am cautious, however, not to suggest that we overthrow the family and substitute other institutions as alternative child-rearers. To do this would be impossible at this stage because of the already mentioned positive value of the family, and because we have not consciously experimented sufficiently with alternatives that could successfully replace it.

Discussion

The creation of alternative life styles, work patterns, or economic change, cannot be successfully imposed on people or prescribed for them without their cooperation. The creation of any alternative processes, when it involves major changes from historical precedent, is a political problem as well as an educational or psycho-social one. For people to attempt alternatives within this society, they must feel the necessity for change and feel that they are not alone in their efforts to create it. People do not attempt to create even small changes in their lives if they lack the confidence or the ability or the power to make them work. In short, programs that would produce the conscious articulation of goals and criteria for positive social change cannot be undertaken without the initiative of the people who are going to be involved.

Acting on the basis of the common sense of oppression experienced by women in society, the women's liberation movement has begun to analyze the relationship between some transitional and long-range goals which, if won, could significantly change women's status in society. The women's liberation movement will not be satisfied, for example, with equality with men if that equality is defined simply in terms of employment opportunity or work status; in present society, that would mean that they give up one oppressive situation (subjugation in the home) to step into another oppressive situation (exploitation at work). Nonetheless, in order for women to participate in efforts to create more meaningful and rewarding work experiences, they must achieve the transitional goal of shared work with men in the home around the housekeeping and child-rearing functions. This means that ways have to be found in which men can begin to take a more active part in home life and in emotional and social interaction with infants. The encouragement of male participation in early childhood socialization requires, for its success, the transformation of existing social and educational institutions because men today are not prepared to assume major shares of responsibility either in home-making or in child-rearing. As Sweden has already done, sex-role stereotyping in books (children's and adult's) and in advertising has to be ended in order to discourage traditional practices of sex-differentiated behavior. Paid paternity leaves for men and greater opportunities for fathers to participate in the care of newborns is recognized as essential. Men have to be involved more in early education, from day-care to primary schools. Unless nurseries and schools are staffed by men as well as women, the responsibility for the socialization of children will continue to fall upon women and they will continue to feel that other social responsibilities are not within their domain. This was apparently the experience of women in the kibbutzim in Israel. At the beginning, women were encouraged to share in the heavy work with men, but men were not similarly encouraged to share in the care of children. As a result, women became overburdened with the strain of both kinds of responsibilities and gradually dropped out of the productive branches. A sexual division of labor persists to this day in the kibbutzim. Only women work as nurses and infant's teachers.(37)

For men and women to share in the care of infants while maintaining jobs, then in their capacity as workers, both men and women have to be able to work shorter hours without losing pay. The extra time would be used for child care either at home or in cooperatively organized day care centers at work or in the community. Group day care is considered by the women's liberation movement to be a more progressive alternative to family day care because it removes children and adults from the isolating and non-productive environment of the home, substituting a social environment in which infants and adults may interact with each other in large, unrestrictive spaces with many objects and toys to share. The socialization process, therefore, becomes less individualistic for the children and more cooperative for the adults. It follows that parental control of the organization and staffing of day care centers is essential. The new, radical generation of parents do not want dumping grounds for their children, but rather centers of exciting educational activity and play in which children and adults share collectively in the process of growing up. Dissatisfied with the racist, sexist, and middle-class-biased education that children receive in public schools, the radical day care movement wants day care that is organized and controlled by the people in their communities who wish to create a more democratic, equalitarian society for their children.(16)

A final word needs to be said about alternatives to the nuclear family, in particular the new movement toward communalism. Seen in the most positive of perspectives, a small percentage of the American population is attempting to establish stable communal living arrangements as a way of socializing productive relationships in the living place. Cooking, shopping, cleaning, child care, and social relationships are being shared by all who live together.

The rennaissance of communalism can be seen to develop out of the women's liberation philosophy. The women's liberation movement helped to convince women that their oppression did not develop from their internal inadequacies, but was the natural outgrowth of problems inherent in the structure of our society. By forming social and political bonds as a group, rather than as individual women, it has been possible for women to experience new and better forms of social relationships and to begin successfully to create some of the changes necessary before all women can, in fact, be liberated. Breaking down alienating forms of social relationships can be seen to be a first step in the process of transforming society. A recent paper on "The Liberation of Children"(2) concludes:

"If we want to change society we can begin by changing the kind of people we are and the kind of children we raise. People who are more loving, more concerned about each other, more secure and less competitive will have attitudes that are contrary to the ones on which our society is based, and while the creation of new attitudes is not in itself a revolution, perhaps it helps create the preconditions."

References

(1) AINSWORTH, M. 1969. Object relations, dependency, and attachment: a theoretical review of the infant-mother relationship. Child Developm. 40:696–1025.

(2) BABCOX, D. 1970. The liberation of children. Up From Under 1(1):43–46 (Up From Under, 339 Lafayette St., New York, N. Y. 10012).

(3) BELL, R. 1971. Stimulus control of parent or caretaker behavior by offspring. Developmental Psychol. 4:63–72. (Invited address, 1968. Division of Developmental Psychological, 76th Annual Convention, American Psychological Association).

(4) BIRCH, H. 1953. Psychology and culture. *In* Basic Problems in Psychiatry, J. Wortis, ed. Grune & Stratton, New York.

(5) BOWLBY, J. 1951. Maternal Care and Mental Health. World Health Organization Monogr., Geneva.

(6) BOWLBY, J. 1961. Foreword. *In* Determinants of Infant Behaviour. B. Foss, ed. Methuen & Co., London.

(7) BOWLBY, J. 1969. Attachment and Loss. Vol. I. Attachment. The Hogarth Press and the Institute of Psychoanalysis, London.

(8) BRUNER, J. 1970. Poverty and Childhood. Paper presented at Merrill-Palmer Institute, Detroit.

(9) CALDWELL, B. ET AL. 1970 Infant day care and attachment. Amer. J. Orthopsychiat. 30:397–412.

(10) CASLER, L. 1961. Maternal deprivation: a critical review of the literature. Monographs Soc. Res. Child Developm. 26(2) ser. #80:1–64.

(11) CHESS, S., THOMAS, A. and BIRCH, H. 1965. Your Child Is A Person. Viking Press, New York.

(12) GAIL, S. 1968. The housewife, *In* Work. R. Fraser, ed. Penguin Books, London.

(13) GAVRON, H. 1968. The Captive Wife. Penguin Books, London. (first published by Routledge & Kegan Paul, London, 1966).

(14) GORDON, L. 1970. Families. New England Free Press, 791 Tremont St., Boston.

(15) GORDON, E. 1971. Parent and child centers: their basis in the behavioral and educational sciences. An invited critique. Amer. J. Orthopsychiat. 41:39—42.

(16) GROSS, L. and MACEWAN, P. 1970. On day care. Women: A Journal of Liberation 1(2):26—29. (Women: A Journal of Liberation, 3011 Guildford Ave., Baltimore, Md. 21218).

(17) HERZOG, E. 1960. Children of Working Mothers. U. S. Dept. of Health, Education and Welfare, Children's Bureau, Washington, D. C.

(18) HOW HARVARD RULES WOMEN. 1970. The Arrogance of social science research: manipulating the lives of black women and their infants. New England Free Press, Boston.

(19) HUNT, J. MC V. 1971. Parent and child centers: Their basis in the behavioral and educational sciences. Amer. J. Orthopsychiat. 41:13—38.

(20) KOTELCHUCK, M. 1971. The nature of the child's tie to the father. Unpublished Ph.D. thesis, Harvard University.

(21) LEHRMAN, D. 1953. A critique of Konrad Lorenz's theory of instinctive behavior. Q. Rev. Biol. 28:337—363.

(22) LORENZ, K. 1935. Companionship in bird life. *In* Instinctive Behavior, C. Schiller, ed., 1957, International Universities Press, New York.

(23) MEAD, M. 1954. Some theoretical considerations on the problem of mother-child separation. Amer. J. Orthopsychiat. 24:471—483.

(24) MEAD, M. 1962. A cultural anthropologist's approach to maternal deprivation. *In* Deprivation of Maternal Care. A Reassessment of its Effects. Public Health Papers, #14, World Health Org., Geneva.

(25) MILLETT, K. 1970. Sexual Politics. Doubleday & Co., New York.

(26) MITCHELL, J. 1966. Women: the longest revolution. New Left Review, 40(Nov-Dec). (Available as a pamphlet from New England Free Press, Boston).

(27) MYRDAL, A. and KLEIN, V. 1968. Women's Two Roles (2nd ed.). Routledge and Kegan Paul, London.

(28) O'CONNOR, N. 1956. The evidence for the permanently disturbing effects of mother-child separation. Acta Psychol. 12:174—191.

(29) ORLANSKY, H. 1949. Infant care and personality. Psychol. Bull. 46:1—48.

(30) PINNEAU, S. 1950. A critique on the articles by Margaret Ribble. Child Developm. 21:203—228.

(31) PINNEAU, S. 1955. The infantile disorders of hospitalism and anaclitic depression. Psychol. Bull. 52:429—452.

(32) PINNEAU, S. 1955. Reply to Dr. Spitz. Psychol. Bull. 52:459—462.

(33) RAPAPORT, R. and RAPAPORT, R. N. 1969. The dual career family: A variant pattern and social change. Human Relations 22:3—30.

(34) REICH, W. 1962. The Sexual Revolution (3rd ed). The Noonday Press (Farrar, Straus and Giroux), New York.

(35) SCHAFFER, H. and EMERSON, P. 1964. The development of social attachments in infancy. Monographs Soc. Res. Child Developm. 29(3):ser. #94.

(36) SCHNEIRLA, T. 1956. Interrelationships of the 'innate' and the 'acquired' in instinctive behavior. *In* L'Instinct Dans le Comportement des Animaux et de l'Homme. P. Grasse, ed. Masson et Cie, Paris.

(37) SPIRO, M. 1965. Children of the Kibbutz. Schocken Books, New York. (First published by Harvard University Press, 1958).

(38) SPITZ, R. 1945. Hospitalism: An inquiry into the genesis of psychiatric conditions in early childhood. Part I. Psychoanal. Stud. Child 1:53—74.

(39) SPITZ, R. and WOLF, K. 1946. Anaclitic depression: an inquiry into the genesis of psychiatric conditions in early childhood (II). Psychoanal. Stud. Child 2:313—342.

(40) STANNARD, U. 1970. Adam's rib, or the woman within. Transaction 8:24—35.

(41) THOMAS, A. ET AL. 1963. Behavioral Individuality in Early Childhood. New York University Press, New York.

(42) TINBERGEN, N. 1951. The Study of Instinct. Clarendon Press, Oxford.

(43) WOOTTEN, B. 1959. Social Science and Social Pathology. Allen and Unwin, London.

(44) YARROW, L. 1961. Maternal deprivation: Toward an empirical and conceptual re-evaluation. Psychol. Bull. 58:459—490.

(45) YARROW, M. ET AL. 1962. Child-rearing in families of working and non-working mothers. Sociometry 25:122—140.

(46) YUDKIN, S. and HOLME, A. 1969. Working Mothers and Their Children. Sphere Books, London. (First published by Michael Joseph, London, 1963).

WHAT DOES EQUALITY
BETWEEN THE SEXES IMPLY?

Birgitta Linnér

Within the context of three possible sex role systems — patriarchal, complementary, and equal — this paper will describe Sweden's current climate of change, and explore new family- and life-styles taking shape as the nation moves closer to equality between the sexes. Contributing to this climate are legal, economic, and social policy, government and education, and public attitudes.

While the goal of equality in all areas of life is now widely accepted, there is still a long way to go. Since no real structural changes can occur among women alone, the focus has broadened to include the situation of men and the question of "men's emancipation." The aim in Sweden is not for a male role or a female role, but for a basically human role.

The steps already taken in Sweden toward equality between the sexes have, of course, produced changes in the psychological relationship between men and women. These changes will be discussed in the areas of marriage and family life, divorce, child-rearing, the men's situation, and sex.

The Three Sex Role Systems

Patriarchal. In the traditional system, men are the providers of the family's needs, and are thus superior; women are economically dependent on — and supplemental to — men. While such a system may be efficient within a family, it carries negative consequences for society.

Complementary. Men and women are regarded as equal, but emphasis remains on their basic differences; they polarize each other. It is a system to which many psychologists cling; Erik Erikson's concept of inner and outer space would seem to be an example. On the other hand, Johan Cullberg,(1) a young psychiatrist at Stockholm's Karoline Hospital, has pointed out that:

> The stereotyped sex roles in our Western culture mean ... that masculinity implies activity, strength, emotional restraint, and dominance. Femininity is defined as passivity, weakness, sentimentality, and submission. ... The man or woman who makes high demands on himself or herself to fulfill these role stereotypes, runs the risk of feeling chronically threatened in self-esteem and possibilities for sexual happiness.

Equality (the human role system). This system acknowledges that differences between the sexes exist, but sees them as secondary and rather uninteresting from the total view that human beings are much more alike than they are different. Thus, it should be possible not merely to create a new, flexible human role in which the same possibilities are open to men and women within the family, in the labor market, and in all other social situations.

Laws And Social Policy

Sweden, in her legal recognition of equality of men and women within the family, stands in contrast to the astonishing number of countries that, although basically democratic, still embody the traditional leadership of the *pater familias* within their systems of law. It is possible for a people to attain economic and emotional equality as long as the subordinate status of married women is maintained in their nation's laws.

The great changes in the structure of Swedish marriage and divorce laws occurred in the first decades of this century. The Marriage and Family Acts of 1915–1920 abolished ties between church and civil laws regarding marriage and sex, and laid the groundwork for the more advanced reform efforts of recent years. They permitted a shift from the male-dominated, hierarchical family toward a family structure based on social and economic equality between husband and wife. Thus, today, if one partner stays at home, he or she is legally regarded as providing economic support for the family. Further, the law makes no distinction as to sex, so that the *hemmaman*, or house-husband, has been legally established in Sweden. Similarly, both partners are equally responsible for the guardianship of their children, and couples may voluntarily agree to divorce without guilt being assigned to either partner.

There have been no illegitimate children in Sweden since 1917, when that term for children born out of wedlock was banned from official usage. Every child born is legal. In 1970, the last vestige of discrimination against out-of-wedlock children was wiped out when they were granted equal paternal inheritance rights with other children. Social attitudes have kept pace with these legal advances. A 1969 report of a government survey(20) showed that 99% of the population feels that all children, born in or out of marriage, should have equal rights; 98% feels that the community should treat unmarried mothers exactly as it treats married mothers; and 16% further declares that since unwed mothers often face greater difficulty in child-rearing, they should be accorded special benefits.

Family planning has been a part of Sweden's public health and welfare program since 1938. It is considered the right of couples to decide whether and when to have children, and the duty of the government to provide counseling and information on contraceptive methods, as well as a fertility program for those who want children. Also in 1938, therapeutic abortion was made legal. (It may be of interest that Sweden today has one of the lowest rates of abortion in the world.)

Homosexuality between consenting adults has not been a criminal offense since 1944, and there is increasing social tolerance and understanding of divergent forms of sexual behavior. In 1962, a new penal code allowed equal and open acceptance of sexuality for men and women, providing it is not damaging to either partner. Premarital sex has been legal for women as well as men since 1915, when a law dating from 1686 was abolished that had required women engaging in premarital sex to pay a penalty of two silver dollars, which went to maintain church property.

Sweden's legal and social policy contains a number of other provisions important to the establishment of equal sex roles. These points, which I have discussed in greater detail elsewhere(8) include an extensive program of prenatal and postnatal care, as well as free delivery; six months maternity leave with pay, and another six months without pay; municipal day care intended not as a substitute for the mother, but as an enrichment for the child; free public schools; equal pay for equal work (although this has not yet been accomplished in practice); and an individual income tax system that has supplanted the former joint, family tax system.

Public Attitudes and Activities

Despite the enlightened laws enacted early in the century to improve the status of women and create equality in marriage, those in control of the institutions of society — the politicians and many of the religious leaders — were successful in maintaining the traditional family role system and the public's adherence to it. It was not until the 1960s that real debate, research, and reform exploded. In 1961, Eva Moberg opened a somewhat confused and emotional debate with the publication of an essay claiming that as long as society demands a double role (work outside and inside the home) from women and a single role from men, equality can never be achieved. Responsibility for home and children must be shared by mother, father, and society, she said, calling for the introduction of the "human role." At the same time, the concept of "sex role," originally used only by sociologists, was taken up by Swedish and Norwegian psychologists and other social scientists.(2) During the early '60s, the "woman question" was abandoned, replaced by the "sex role question" that embodied the idea that the role of women could not be viewed separately from that of men.

In Sweden, it was not only the angry young rebels who challenged the validity of the traditional family system in the '60s. Questions, such as those explored in recent research by Harriet Holter(5) on biological as opposed to cultural roots of sex differences, were taken up early and seriously by newspapers, magazines, radio, and television. Further, all major labor unions and political parties take the position that there should be equality between the sexes in all areas of life, and all agree that it is not a question of single reforms but of restructuring society.

In the mid-'60s, consideration was first given to the concept of male emancipation. Due to the imbalance in the traditional role system, men have taken on the entire burden of supporting the family, have been deprived of emotional contact with their children, and are weighed down with responsibility that often leads to serious physical and psychological disturbances. Men have a higher rate than women of ulcer problems, heart disease, early death, suicide, crime, and alcoholism.

The debate on equality between the sexes has become to some extent a political issue. Some believe that capitalism and the patriarchal society are close companions; one leading spokesman for this radical view maintains that the sex role movement of the '60s has become watered down ideologically and has stagnated. Eva Moberg(12) replied to this position as follows:

> I have never claimed that there is no connection between capitalism and [male-dominated society]! There are . . . many threads between them. But I do not believe that the one is a direct consequence of the other, or that socialism is any guarantee whatsoever against sex discrimination . . . I believe that social conditions and the human psyche are interwoven into one another reciprocally. That's why I also believe that − in the case of such a relatively open and free society as Sweden nonetheless is − society can be changed in crucial and profound ways through continuous reform work. A revolution on the other hand must wage constant warfare, after its dear victory . . . *to preserve itself.*

Personally, I think it is unfortunate that the sex role question, an issue of basic human rights, be made mainly a political issue.

Among Sweden's women's organizations currently striving for equality, one of the more prominent is Group 8. It might be interesting to compare the goals and demands of Group 8 with those of women's liberation groups in the United States, in order to get some indication of the stages of development of the movement for equality in the two countries.

The Group 8 manifesto, which maintains that "even if women manage to gain equality with men, they will not be free . . . before men are also free," calls for: 1) legal right to the same working conditions as men; 2) unemployment insurance and free adult education for all women who apply for but do not get work; 3) educational assistance for adult students, regardless of spouse's level of income; 4) laws protecting part-time personnel; 5) day care for all children between six months and seven years old, backed by unemployment insurance for mothers who cannot work because of lack of nurseries; 6) free abortion, with the right − but not the obligation − to consult a social worker, and free contraceptives for men and women; and 7) the assignment of 25% of all new housing to collectives.

Government

The Swedish government is quick to absorb and promote new attitudes arising out of public debate and economic, social, and medical research. For example, the idea of men's emancipation was stressed by the government in a 1968 report to the United Nations on the Status of Women in Sweden,(18) probably the first time a government has taken the men's situation, as well as the women's, into official consideration:

> A decisive and ultimately durable improvement in the status of women cannot be attained by special measures aimed at women alone; it is equally necessary to abolish the conditions which tend to assign certain privileges, obligations or rights to men. No decisive change in the distribution of functions and status . . . between the sexes can be achieved if the duties of the male in society are assumed *a priori* to be unaltered. The aim of reform work in this area must be to change the traditional division of labour which tends to deprive women of the possibility of exercising their legal rights on equal terms. The division of functions . . . between the sexes must be changed in such a way that both the man and the woman in a family are afforded the same practical opportunities of participating in both active parenthood and gainful employment.

The involvement of the marriage and family lawmakers in the present reforms to establish equality was admitted officially in August 1969, when the Minister of Justice, in a directive to the governmental commission established to overhaul the present family law, said:

> . . . legislation is one of the most essential instruments which society possesses for meeting . . . people's desires or for channeling development into new paths . . . The transition from old to new should be made with care and consideration for individual people, but there is no reason to abstain from using marriage and family legislation as one of several instruments in reform efforts toward a society where every adult individual can take responsibility for himself without being economically dependent on relatives and where equality between men and women is a reality.

There is interest in the equality process on the municipal, as well as the federal level. In my home town, Uppsala, the program of the Social

Democrats includes improvement of child care facilities because:

> A speedy expansion of childcare is an important means for
> increased equality between children from different home
> environments, between single and two-parent families, be-
> tween high and low wage-earners, and between women and
> men. . . . A speedy expansion of day-care centers, led and
> controlled by the community, is needed to further guaran-
> tee all children security and stable care and to enable all
> parents, especially single and low income parents, to fend
> for themselves and to increase their standard of living by
> their own work.

Education

The educational system is one of the most important instruments in
creating equality between the sexes, as it is in creating equality between
different social, economic, and geographical groups. Sweden's nine-year
comprehensive school, coeducational as is all other education and
training (except military training), incorporates the ideas of emancipation from traditional sex roles. Since 1962, when the new public school
system was introduced, boys have been taught such traditionally
feminine, role-dividing subjects as home economics, sewing, and child-
care. Girls learn modern manual handicraft and other once exclusively
masculine skills.

Textbooks are continually being revised and updated to promote the
concept of equal sex roles in all areas of life. The latest curriculum,
promulgated by the National Board of Education for the '70s, is even
more positive and progressive in regard to the sex role issue. Information on sex role questions will be provided in all grades and in various
subjects. Pupils will be encouraged to discuss and question differences
between men and women in terms of influence and salary, as well as in
family life. This emphasis on equality will, of course, be included in
teacher training.

In discussing these questions with students in the schools, I have
found that boys and girls enjoy these themes; they feel the injustices
that exist in society, and they are open for re-orientating themselves,
both in professional life and in family life. In addition, the boys seem
to be showing a new concern for the care of children.

Research On Equality

At the Scandinavian Seminar for Sex Role Research, sex differentiation and the effects of sex roles are being studied in collaboration with colleagues from the other Scandinavian countries. Various government agencies and universities are also conducting surveys.

At the university level, an extension course on sex roles at Uppsala University offers classes in, "The Fight for Franchise in Sweden: In Reality and Literature," "Men's Roles in Some Modern Swedish Literary Works," and "Is There Sex Discrimination in Our Academic Textbooks?" In regard to the last, medical texts in obstetrics and gynecology might well be singled out for their prejudices against women.

At Goethenburg University Library, there is a Woman's History archive, where research on the history of women and on modern sex role problems is collected and catalogued. University research projects in such areas as social anthropology, economic history, church history, literature, psychology, law, and sociology are included in the archive, as are labor union research and projects devoted to the sex role question.

New Life Styles

Various types of family and cooperative living arrangements have become accepted in Sweden, including one-parent families, communes, and weekend marriages. A new trial marriage has evolved, in which a couple sets out to see if they can cooperate in everyday life, and if their relationship is emotionally solid enough for them to have children. Other young people may choose either legal or "loyalty" marriages, whichever seems most suitable to their needs.

Sweden's social welfare program accepts different patterns of co-living and various family styles. In civil law, however, only registered marriages are valid. Since many young people have adopted one of the newer informal marital relationship patterns, a government commission has been appointed to find forms for legalizing different marital and family styles. According to Sweden's Minister of Justice, "The functions of legislation in this connection is to solve practical problems, not to privilege one form of living together above others."

Since the new family concepts are of wide general interest, they are given considerable space in the nation's mass media. However, there are some who feel that more attention is needed. In a 1969 interview in the

Stockholm newspaper *Expressen*, a woman who characterized her experiences in communal living as "more love, less fear, less egoism," went on to say:

> The practical problems are legion. No one builds communal family flats ... even though it would be economically profitable for society to invest in [them].... The communal family is simply not a common alternative yet, just as adoption is not a common alternative ... despite the fact that there are hundreds of thousands of children without parents. This is where the mass media have a responsibility, which they of course have shirked. A constructive debate, information and analysis could have made the communal family alternative of interest [to] city planners and architects, building firms, social scientists, and the ordinary man in the street.

Psychological Issues

With our society paving the way for equality, we must consider what a high degree of equality means for the psychodynamics of interpersonal relationships. I will discuss some aspects of the changing content of the man-woman relationship from the viewpoint of my experiences as a marriage counselor.

Marital problems. In the traditional marriage, the wife lives through her husband, demanding that he make her happy and give her status. He must be the breadwinner for the family. This unbalanced economic structure can easily create an unbalanced psychological structure, particularly observable at critical moments in the relationship.

For a couple with legal, economic, philosophical, and practical equality, there is available a new type of dynamic process with which to work through an emotional crisis. Each partner has his or her identity, and there is no need to place blame on one partner, as there tends to be in a superior-inferior relationship. The more role-fixated and unbalanced a relationship is, the more tempting it is to project one's own faults and frustrations onto one's partner, and to create guilt feelings. When there is equality and self-esteem, it is easier to accept one's own responsibility in a conflict and to find solutions humiliating to neither party. Of course, all problems do not disappear, but the possibilities of working them out are greater when the man and woman are equal.

Divorce. False dependency easily leads to neurotic crisis situations, especially in divorce, where there is often much bitterness, aggressiveness, anxiety, and guilt. With equality between the spouses and with a rational law system that accepts divorce between consenting adults, the possibilities for psychological destruction during the divorce proceedings are greatly reduced.

If the divorce occurs between equals, the children have a better chance of being able to love both parents. Though the marriage has failed, there is no need for the partners to point to each other as guilty, cruel, or unfaithful. If marriage is to be a meaningful psychological relationship, not merely an economic arrangement, simpler divorce laws entailing less dramatic proceedings are a definite requirement. When divorce is no longer considered a crime, but merely a rational means of dissolving a contract, then there will be possibilities for mature dissolutions of bad marriages.

Children. Female and male identity, long tied rigidly to the bearing and supporting of children, is finally being freed from these traditional roles. In fact, young people today often decide not to have children, or to adopt them, rather than add to an already overpopulated world. But what about the effects of the new, equal family upon the children? Is the child made insecure when the father does the housework and the child care? Or when the parents or work-sharing couple share the duties, both at home and in the labor market? Will there emerge a new sex-identity, or a lack of such identity, among the children of these modern parents? There are many such unanswered questions. But, as one child psychologist recently put it to me, it is difficult to believe that identification with more harmonious and mature adult personalities will not have positive consequences for the children. We may get new personality types, but why be afraid of that?

Since young people today openly accept equal sexuality, they are better able to make candid and reasoned decisions as to whether or not to have children. Married women are no longer under the social pressures they once were to have children, more or less automatically. Modern contraceptive techniques also help to realize this healthier and more mature approach, in which having a baby is now more often an accurate reflection of mutual emotional desire on the part of the couple concerned. This freedom of choice is an indication of greater maturity, and children are less likely to be used as outlets for marital frustrations.

Men. What happens to the man as the new equality threatens the bastion of his supremacy? What happens when the decision-making positions in business and politics are no longer reserved exclusively for men, but are open to the qualified regardless of sex? When it is no longer taken for granted that the man is the erotic initiative-taker, and the one who makes the important family decisions and is thereby released from common household chores? How will he manage, how will he take it emotionally?

Certainly, in this transitional stage, there are problems for men. Having been brought up in a male-oriented society, men do not dare to share emotions and closeness with women on equal terms. The solution lies in women and men together conceptualizing what mutuality in a personal relationship means. We have to remember that, as women have been deprived of responsibility in society, men have been deprived emotionally, and have therefore been prone to stagnate as emotional beings.

It is interesting to observe how young men absorb the new male emancipation, as the society begins to move in a direction in which it will not be demeaning to the man to do housework or child care. Expectant fathers are now taking part in child care courses. More and more hospitals are allowing fathers to be present and assist in the delivery of their children, and many of these young fathers are experiencing new depths of emotion during the experience. Thus, increasingly, men seem to like taking part in child care and the practical and emotional responsibility of bringing up children.

Family life. One of the most frequent questions raised is whether the new equality will destroy family life. It is important to emphasize that flexibility does not mean a breakdown of family structure. As one couple living as a new *equality-family* put it, if family structure means that the woman cleans the house and caters to the man, then our family has broken down. But, they add, for us this new family style means more harmonious and creative interrelations, wider range of common interests and communications, and greater chance for fulfillment in family life.

Thus, with the emphasis of family life on full, all-around development of the individual, the new equality offers better grounds for a healthy start in life for children, and for enriched stable relations between man and woman.

Sex. Masters and Johnson have given scientific validity to facts that were hidden or ignored for centuries, as society denied women the rights to their own sexuality. The demonstration that women are capable of sexual pleasure and satisfaction to the same degree as men will be very important in changing the rigid attitudes toward women's sex life, and meaningful relationships in the future.

Under the new equal role system, sexual satisfaction carries less guilt and becomes more meaningful and enjoyable than previously. When a couple has good sex relations, infidelity becomes correspondingly less interesting and tempting. The most recent publication(19) of the government's Commission for Sex Education has proposed as a basic sex education ethic that men's and women's sex behavior must be judged equally, and that all reasoning based on women not being equal to men must be dismissed.

Conclusion

Sweden found a champion for the cause of women's emancipation as early as 1793 in the poet Thomas Thorild, whose essay on "The Natural Dignity of the Female Sex" upheld women's right to be regarded, first of all, as human beings, and only secondly as females. Now, nearly two hundred years later, there is still much to be done. But a dynamic process of change is underway. What I have tried to show, if only sketchily, is that this movement toward equality between man and woman is to no one's detriment, and to everyone's benefit. The aim is for a new role-balance allowing greater personal independence and integrity, and opening new possibilities for mature and harmonious relationships. As men and women continue to free themselves from misconceptions about the other sex, we will begin to evolve a more human society for both.

References and Related Reading

(1) CULLBERG, J. 1970. Medical aspects of gender identity. Paper presented at seminar on Planned Parenthood and Sex Education in Sweden, April 1970. Division of Population and Family Welfare, Swedish International Development Authority, Stockholm.

(2) DAHLSTRÖM, E., ed. 1967. The Changing Roles of Men and Women. Duckworth, London.

(3) FREDRIKSSON, I. 1969. The future role of women. Futures (Dec. 1969). ILIFFENTP, Inc., 330 E. 42nd St., New York.

(4) GRØNSETH, E. 1970. The dysfunctionality of the husband-provider role in industrialized societies. Paper presented at the VIIth World Congress of Sociology, Family Research Session, Verna, Bulgaria. (Author's address: Institute of Sociology, Oslo University, Oslo, Norway.)

(5) HOLTER, H. 1970. Sex Roles and Social Structure. Universitetsförlaget, Oslo. (In U. S.: Box 142, Boston, Mass. 02113.)

(6) LEIJON, A. 1968. Swedish Women-Swedish Men. The Swedish Institute, Stockholm. (P. O. Box 7072, S-103 82 Stockholm, Sweden.)

(7) LINNÉR, B. 1968. The sexual revolution in Sweden. *In* Impact of Science on Society, vol. XVIII, no. 4. UNESCO, Paris.

(8) LINNÉR, B. 1972. Sex and Society in Sweden, 1967, 2nd Ed. 1972, Harper Colophon Books, New York.

(9) LINNÉR, B. 1966. Sexual morality and sexual reality: the Scandinavian approach. Amer. J. Orthopsychiat. 36(4):686–693.

(10) LINNÉR, B. 1965. Society and Sex in Sweden. Swedish Institute for Culture Relations, Stockholm.

(11) LINNÉR, B. 1965. Family planning in Sweden. U. S. Senate Hearings on Population Crisis, Part 2-B, pp. 1282–1292.

(12) MOBERG, E. 1971. VI (no. 3), Stockholm.

(13) MYRDAL, A. 1968. Nation and Family. MIT Press, Cambridge, Mass.

(14) MYRDAL, A. and KLEIN, V. 1968. Women's Two Roles (2nd ed.). Routledge & Kegan Paul, London.

(15) PALME, O. 1970. The emancipation of man. Address to the Women's National Democratic Club, Washington, D. C. (June 8, 1970). Available from Swedish Embassy, 2249 R St. NW, Washington, D. C., 20008.

(16) REPORT BY THE GOVERNMENT OF SWEDEN TO THE UNITED NATIONS. 1970. Family Planning and the Status of Women in Sweden. No. 3. Ministry of Health and Social Affairs, Stockholm.

(17) REPORT BY THE LO COUNCIL FOR FAMILY QUESTIONS. 1970. The Trade Unions and the Family. Stockholm.

(18) REPORT TO THE UNITED NATIONS. 1968. The Status of Women in Sweden. The Swedish Institute, Stockholm.

(19) SEX EDUCATION COMMISSION. 1971. Sexuality and Relationships: Facts and Points of View for Sex Education. (In Swedish.)

(20) SEX EDUCATION COMMISSION. 1969. Swedish Sexual Norms and Sexual Behaviour. SOU (2) Om sexuallivet i Sverige. (In Swedish.)

(21) TROST, J. 1970. Adultery in Sweden. FF3, Department of Sociology. The Group for Family Research, Drottninggatan 1A, S-752 20 Uppsala, Sweden.

(22) THE JOURNAL HERTHA. 1969. No. 5. Fredrika Bremer Association, Biblioteksgatan 12, S-111 46 Stockholm, Sweden. ($1.00)

CHANGES IN THE MODERN FAMILY:
THEIR IMPACT ON SEX ROLES

Janet Zollinger Giele

We have just passed through an era, lasting roughly from 1920 to 1960, in which women were extraordinarily satisfied with and optimistic about their status. There was, in some circles, a derisive attitude toward the feminists of an earlier era who had been aggressive in the cause of winning equal political rights for themselves. During that recent period it took an intellectual effort to remember that female suffragists had to *fight* against considerable *opposition* to accomplish their goal.

In 1971 the mood has changed. College students who five years ago showed no interest in the status of women (although they were very much interested in the problems of blacks) are today demanding and getting courses on the history, sociology, psychology, and literature of women. Betty Friedan's(6) *The Feminine Mystique* commands more attention now than when it first appeared in 1963. The women's movement is a topic of interest even to the mass media. And since *Sexual Politics*(13) appeared, more women are wary of "patriarchal" domination by men. Furthermore, some people are now broadening the question of sex roles to take issue with the whole structure of the nuclear family, particularly with the division of labor that makes the husband the sole provider and keeps the wife at home in charge of the children.

The Problem

The question I wish to pose is this: Why do we find this new *consciousness* emerging, critical of women's status and the relationship between the sexes?

The easy answer is that women have been converted to the feminist cause. Such an explanation assumes that the ideology of a Kate Millet, once it has been developed and propagated, is irresistible. But this is hardly satisfying, for it fails to account for the relative lack of response to Simone de Beauvoir's(3) powerful statement, *The Second Sex*, which appeared in America in 1952.

A more satisfying approach looks to deeper changes in process in the society, which have laid a foundation for a change of consciousness in those born since 1930. It is in these generations that we see budding interest in the new feminism and in possible new forms of family life.

Some Alternative Theories

Previous explanations of the relation between the sexes have generally been of three sorts, ascribing the main cause of change or stability to technology, ideology, or the division of labor. Each provides elements of an explanatory theory, but any one, taken alone, cannot satisfactorily account for the current burst of consciousness.

The technological theory of change, long associated with the name of W. F. Ogburn(12) in sociology, points to labor-saving devices, improved contraception, better health and longer life span as some of the important factors that have freed women from the family and contributed to the rise in their labor force participation. Such a theory explains a gradual increase in percent of women working, but it explains neither the quiescence of the 1950s nor the angry outburst of the late 1960s.

The ideological theory of change represented by Friedan or Millet points to subtle attitudes that allow men to dominate women. But taken alone, it cannot account for the emergence of a new consciousness which rejects patriarchy and the feminine mystique.

Parsons and Bales(17) have developed a more complete theoretical position that could encompass both technology and values by focusing on the division of labor. According to their theory, American men and women together value equality of opportunity and achievement, but their roles are different: Men achieve in work outside the home; women cultivate the opportunity of the child to realize his full potential by staying inside the home. Though this theory provided an adequate interpretation for the 1950s, it did not foresee the turmoil we now observe.

Consciousness and the Universalization of Sex Roles

The fault of Parsons and Bales' analysis was that it froze men's and women's roles at one point in time, while in fact those roles were changing with the increasing complexity of the surrounding social structure. Had they applied the theory of their Chapter VII to the evolution of adult sex roles, they would have avoided this difficulty.

When a society becomes more complex, roles become more specialized, or differentiated. That is, a job is broken down into several different operations, some of which may be performed by the person who originally did the whole job, some of which may be taken over by experts who perform only newly specialized functions.

When a job is broken up like this (*i.e.,* differentiated), two other things happen at the same time. First, parts of the job can now be performed by persons who under the old rule were not qualified. Second, the very fact of breaking up the job into component parts has an effect on the consciousness of all the people involved: they become aware that certain qualifications they once thought intrinsically necessary to the performance of the job are not in fact so, at least not for certain parts of the operation. As a result the original role, which was seen to be segmentally related to others around it, is now seen as an *integral* made up of several components, a number of which are like the components in other units. Thus is built the possibility of a *shared consciousness* — a sense of commonality or of universal qualities in persons and roles that were initially felt to be totally different from each other. It was a similar process that Marx and Engels described when they observed the relation between the introduction of the factory system and the emergence of class consciousness. (My analysis of the differentiation process owes much to a theoretical formulation by Talcott Parsons in *Societies* [Prentice-Hall, 1966], pp. 21–24.)

If the change in men's and women's roles is a process of differentiation with its greater potential for recognizing human qualities that are shared across the sexes, then it should be possible to identify forces in the larger society that have served to split up traditional sex roles into several component parts, allowing some previously performed by only one sex to be carried out by persons with requisite qualifications without regard to sex.

It is my thesis that such a process of differentiation has been going on in men's and women's roles. Women's work such as cooking has been routinized and rationalized to a point that a man can put a load of laundry in the dryer or a frozen dinner in the oven as well as any woman. Similarly, men's work is less and less tied to physical strength in which presumably males excel, and women are therefore able to do many of the manual, clerical, or intellectual operations that men do. The upshot is that a cross-over is possible in many aspects of role performance that were formerly linked to sex. Consequently, a shared consciousness is possible in which men and women can perceive more clearly each other's problems and satisfactions, and as a result identify with each other.

Institutional Changes

Such an outcome is not due to changed technology alone. If it were, we would be hard pressed to explain why sex roles received so little attention only a few years ago, when admittedly technology had already made great strides. Important changes have also been occurring in more subtle aspects of the sexual division of labor such as child care and the nature of family life. I shall argue that, roughly since the 1930s, relevant changes have occurred in four major institutional areas of the society that have had a formative influence on the generations born since then and have laid the foundations for a revolution of consciousness about sex roles that is just beginning to emerge.

These changes occurred in 1) the relation of the individual to the accepted moral code; 2) the relation of the individual to the family; 3) the relation of family to government; and 4) the relation of the family to the economy.

In each of these areas, I shall describe two phases of functional differentiation that have set the stage for change in attitudes about sex roles. The first phase is a process of *specialization* in which one primary concern is selected. The second phase is a process of *inclusion* in which other necessary functions are also identified as worthy of attention. As a result of both these processes *universalization of consciousness* becomes possible.

Changes in the Moral Code

The first important institutional change was based on discovery of a new basis of morality, initially apparent in sexual conduct, later in other moral issues. Moral changes were significant for family and sex roles because they could transform general assumptions about the boundaries between behavior appropriate to youth and adults, to single and married people, and to men and women.

Specialization of the sexual function as expression of individuality. The central theme of the sexual revolution has been a change in standards of premarital chastity. As Reiss(18) has pointed out, the rates of non-virginity at marriage have changed little since the 1920s. What has changed is the acceptance of premarital intercourse if it occurs within the context of affection.(32)

Sexual mores changed because sexuality came to be regarded as *the* means of individual self-expression and gratification if it occurred in the context of a continuing relationship. As such, sexual intercourse gained legitimacy outside marriage and apart from its reproductive aspect. It was available to youth as well as to adults. Although technical improvements in contraception facilitated this change, they alone do not account for it, for the exercise of sexual intercourse was regulated not by technology or traditional authority but by consideration for the feelings of the individuals involved.

Inclusion of self-expression and the New Morality in moral transformation. Once the sexual function had been differentiated from the total married adult state, it became apparent that performance of other aspects of adult life might also be subjected to redefinition. In the 1960s, young people began to experiment with other than sexual forms of expression – drugs and the hippie style. Youth also gave expression to a new kind of moral concern for war, peace, and responsible exercise of authority in universities, industry, and the military. SNCC, the Peace Corps, and Vista all voiced a moral purpose in areas once thought the sole province of adults.

Universalization of sexual and moral consciousness. The consequence of moral transformation was the emergence of youth as a distinct stage in the life cycle, a period when boys and girls could, as Keniston(11) has said "acknowledge both self and society, personality and social process, without denying the claims of either." By such a standard, sexuality could occur outside marriage; responsible moral positions could be argued by persons who are not yet adults.

Significantly, at each stage of the moral revolution, *both men and women have been involved.* Women have been allowed to become as sexually expressive as men had earlier been. Young men have become as morally concerned with peace and community well-being as were women of Jane Addams's era. The result has been new consciousness of universal qualities shared between the sexes.

Psychology and Family Life

While the sexual revolution and the emergence of youth clarified the nature of responsible moral and sexual behavior *outside* the family, new attitudes about child-rearing clarified the central activities occurring *within* the family. Later still came concern with the development of adult personality. The outcome of these changes was a new sensitivity to the question of whether the family as it is presently constituted can serve the needs of individual men and women.

Specialization of the family in child-care. Following as they did the loss of important productive functions from the home, the decades of the 1920s and 1930s saw a concentration on the child-rearing functions of the family. The goal was to bring up children able to live in a peaceful and democratic world, capable of cooperation and self-direction, and not merely obedient to authority. To this end the whole child development movement was oriented.(5) By the end of the depression, nursery schools, permeated by these ideas and linked to efforts at parent education, had spread across the country. The new ideas were followed most closely by the middle classes, but by the late 1950s there was evidence that even working class parents had felt the effects.(1)

Initially the mother was seen as the expert in child-rearing. She was more open to the new ideas, while the father might revert to being "heavy-handed." Gradually, however, the importance of the father's role was also recognized. In 1939, L. K. Frank(4) wrote,

> While the mother is largely responsible for the child's patterns of intimacy, the father is primarily responsible for the child's ideals of social conduct and his major aspirations and ambitions toward the social world.

Thus eventually *both* mother and father were seen as important in child-rearing.

Inclusion of concern for development of adults. While at first the special function of the family was seen as child-rearing, in recent years the marital role has been singled out for increased attention.(7) Perhaps it is because child-rearing is bunched in the early years of marriage that more attention is given the needs of adults who continue in the family. Perhaps, also, husband and wife now need to find greater satisfaction in each other because their high mobility has uprooted them from single sex social networks that supported them in the past.

Whatever the dynamics of this development, its consequences have been more striking for women than for men. Women are now demanding that the home serve their individual needs for self-realization as much as it appears to serve the husband (by letting him do his work in peace and providing rest and recreation at the end). They protest the "shitwork" that constantly serves others' needs and not their own.(31) In their demand is the belief that the home should be a place that facilitates women's personal growth rather than a prison of stagnation.

Universalization of parental and marital roles. If child-rearing and stabilization of adult personality are identified as the special functions of the family, the structure of the family has to become more flexible. During the early years of married life child-rearing will predominate and sex roles may diverge sharply. Later a couple may devote themselves to common interests such as travel or life in a retirement village in which their roles become more similar. Such flexibility is not unknown to us now. It may eventually result in more widespread questioning of traditional family patterns. Today among the avant garde, alternative forms of child care (day care, etc.) and marriage (serial or communal) are already being considered and tried out.

Government Policy toward the Family

Simultaneous with the evolution of a new sexual ethic and deepening awareness of the psychological significance of the family, there has been a gradual and at times painful effort to formulate government policy toward the family. Initially, in the 1930s, the concern of government was to ensure support of children under conditions of depression and unemployment. During the 1960s, however, government concern broadened to consider the problem of maintaining incentive for work, and proposals for a negative income tax and family allowances were put forward. Despite considerable resistance to these proposals, I believe we are on the threshold of an era when the family's crucial contribution to the formation and maintenance of responsible citizens in a free society will be publicly recognized.

Specialization of family support to aid dependent children. The crisis of the depression created a distinction in the public mind between adults' economic roles and their family responsibilities. It was recognized that persons might be unemployed through no fault of their own and yet have families whose lives depended on their work. A patchwork of insurance, pension, and Social Security programs developed to provide for the young, the old, and the infirm.(27) Of these the most relevant to family change was AFDC, Aid to Families with Dependent Children, established under Title IV of the Social Security Act.

During the 1930s, governmental support of the family identified the child-rearing function as being of special importance. And again, as in the child psychology of the era, the mother was seen as the specialist who could carry on this activity more or less alone if she and her children were provided with support.

Inclusion of the incentive problem in family support. In the 1960s, however, with the discovery of poverty in the midst of an affluent society, and the recognition that a disproportionate number of draft rejects were children who had received AFDC, there was a new willingness to recognize the hazards of father absence and the self-perpetuating cycle of dependence. The Moynihan Report and ensuing proposals for a negative income tax and family allowances pointed to the necessity of assuring fathers jobs (or compensation commensurate with their family responsibilities) so that they would not desert and would instead maintain incentive to support their families and fulfill the important paternal role.(14)

In 1968, Moynihan(28) wrote, "Men are paid for the work they perform on the job, not for the role they occupy in the family." But his point was that they should be paid for that too. He had earlier argued that it would save the government money to ensure fathers jobs and foster stable family life, rather than later have to rehabilitate disadvantaged children by expensive government programs.(14)

Universalization of family consciousness across sex and class lines. It is easy to see conditions for one kind of universalization of consciousness emerging that recognizes that *both* men and women are important to family life and that children can suffer from *pa*ternal deprivation as well as *ma*ternal deprivation.

But the storm that the Moynihan report raised suggests that another kind of universalization is also occurring — albeit haltingly and painfully. This is a sharing of consciousness across class, ethnic, and racial groups. Blacks bitterly protested the Moynihan report because they thought it was saying that one kind of family, the white, middle-class, "intact" family was best. Actually their protest may point to an enlarged consciousness of the future that will assert that it is not important which person (mother, father, or other family member) performs the provider role, or performs the parental function. What may instead be the crucial question in the future is simply, are these functions being performed adequately?

The Family in an Affluent Economy

Government policy toward the family is gradually moving away from an implicitly anti-natalist policy that gives only minimal support to the poor, to a policy of universal family allowances that would be neither pro-natalist nor anti-natalist but would give compensation for performance of parental functions. This still leaves open the question of population control. In the 1950s, women chose to have a third or fourth child to fill the time left free by diminishing household tasks. In the 1960s there is growing awareness that women may better use their leisure by taking a job outside the home, thereby making not only a productive contribution to the economy but also a step toward control of population.

Specialization of the household in consumption. The striking achievement of the affluent society has been elimination of toil within the household. Seeley(19) and Whyte(30) in their accounts of suburbs in the 1950s both note the acquisition of new household appliances and the kind of "managerial" role the housewife performed as she coordinated the purchase and serving of packaged foods, the care of household and clothing, and the scheduling of her own and her family's activities. Gone is the 19th century pattern of hours spent sewing, cleaning, baking or gardening.(21) These activities are now done by *choice*, for ready-made articles are easily bought. The modern housewife's specific function is to consume rather than to produce. And it is the woman who is seen as the expert in home management.

Her life is not always satisfying, however. Seeley found that "many a Crestwood mother, while 'accepting' the culturally approved maternal role, reveals an underlying resentment." One "creative" solution was to have more children.(10) Another was to invest more time in their care. Van Bortel(29) found in 1953 that homemakers used about as many hours in cooking and housework as they had in the late 1920s. But they spent nearly twice as many hours in "caring for the family."

Inclusion of occupation in the choice of alternatives. By the beginning of the 1960s, however, there were indications that the baby boom would not last forever and that the choice of outside employment was an increasingly accepted alternative. In an affluent society where the ideal is to do work that is interesting and satisfying, not tiring or boring,(7) it is understandable that women would frequently choose the satisfactions of employment over the sometimes less satisfying routines of housework. But, in addition, women's work might bring extra money into households, not as in the past to cover the bare necessities, but to further new and higher goals of consumption.

Universalization of family planning and commitment to occupation. As the household conveniences of the affluent society have grown, women have had more choice in how they will spend their time, and they have come into more control of consumer decisions than they have ever had before. Among all such decisons, perhaps the most far-reaching has to do with family size. The number and spacing of children determines the time and resources that will be available for other uses. Women liberationists currently emphasize the right of women to control their own bodies and their right to easy contraception and abortion. But generally, I believe, our emerging desire for population control implies that not just the woman but each couple will engage in rational planning about family size and that the outcome will be the result of a *joint decision.* Thus the issue of family planning is universalized to touch the consciousness of both men and women.

As more women enter paid employment, the possibility arises for another kind of exchange of consciousness between men and women. On the one hand, women may learn to share with men the frustrations and demands, as well as the stimulations, of occupation. On the other hand, women may be able to teach men how better to integrate work and family by arguing for parttime work, more flexible hours, parent leaves — all of which can relieve some of the strain on the working man as well as on the working woman.

Demographic Trends

Recent changes in rates of marriage, child-bearing, and employment of women all suggest that parental and marital roles have been differentiated so that they are no longer seen as coterminous with women's lives. Since the 1940s, more women are free to combine activities that were once thought to be mutually exclusive. Like men, they are free to do several things at once: marry, have children, *and* work.

A key factor in this change has been the shortening of the child-bearing period. Beginning with the 1920s the average number of children per family dropped to 3.5. This factor,(22) combined with earlier marriage, resulted in the average woman bearing her last child by the age of 26. Clearly a great deal of her time was set free for other activities.

A second key development has been the drop in number of people who remain single. The change was most striking during the 1940s among highly educated women for whom the rate of change was twice that of the general population.(8) Given that a higher proportion of college-educated women work than those with less education, the combined effect of those trends was to bring more married women into the labor force. However, it was probably this same increase in marriage rate that also accounted for the drop in percent of women receiving advanced degrees after 1940.(25)

A third significant shift was in the employment rate of mothers with young children, which more than doubled in the years between 1948 and 1967.(23) That such an increase could occur during a period of general affluence suggests a remarkable reorganization of marital and parental roles. Women had time, energy, and motivation to fulfill several kinds of obligations at once, perhaps because housework, child rearing, marriage, and occupation were all specific and limited enough in their demands to permit such integration.

Conclusion

Change in the family, demographic trends, and new consciousness about sex roles are linked. Institutional change impinging on the family facilitated women's entry into the labor force. At the same time, actual changes in men's and women's behavior undoubtedly influenced the mores of family life. But this two-way relationship does not in itself explain the *sudden* rise of consciousness about sex roles in the late 1960s.

The fact that the great majority of women in the current liberation movement were born since 1930 is suggestive here. Perhaps it was only when these generations had come of age that a concerted assault on traditional family roles could take place. These younger people had been steeped in the new morality, the new psychology, the experience of mechanization and the interchangeability of personnel. It took only a small step to extend these principles to sex roles.

Change will require a much larger step from older generations and people unfamiliar or unsympathetic with these trends. The elements of a stereotyped sex role ideology are still very much with us. Nevertheless, it is not amiss to suggest that there may be a more rapid acceptance of sex equality *in principle* (as distinguished from all aspects of behavior) than is presently supposed. For it is after all not only the generation under forty that has experienced post-depression changes, but the whole society. If people can be shown that liberation of men and women is not a wild idea but an extension of reasonable principles they have already accepted, and in fact *lived*, then it is only a matter of time until we shall see further change of remarkable proportions.

References

(1) BRONFENBRENNER, U. 1958. Socialization and social class through time and space. *In* Readings in Social Psychology, 3rd ed., E. Maccoby, T. Newcomb and E. Hartley, eds. Holt, New York.

(2) CLAUSEN, J. 1968. A historical and comparative view of socialization theory and research. *In* Socialization and Society, J. Clausen, ed. Little Brown, Boston.

(3) DE BEAUVOIR, S. 1952. The Second Sex. Modern Library, New York.

(4) FRANK, L. 1939. The father's role in child nurture. Child Study 16(March):135–136.

(5) FRANK, L. 1962. The beginnings of child development and family life education in the twentieth century. Merrill-Palmer Quart. 8(July):207–227.

(6) FRIEDAN, B. 1963. The Feminine Mystique. Norton, New York.

(7) GALBRAITH, J. 1958. The Affluent Society. Houghton Mifflin, Boston.

(8) GLICK, P. 1957. American Families. Wiley, New York.

(9) HILL, R. and ALDOUS, J. 1969. Socialization for marriage and parenthood. *In* Handbook of Socialization Theory and Research, D. Goslin, ed. Rand-McNally, New York.

(10) HOFFMAN, L. and WYATT, F. 1960. Social change and motivations for having larger families: some theoretical considerations. Merrill-Palmer Quart. 6(July):235–244.

(11) KENISTON, K. 1968. Young Radicals. Harcourt Brace, New York.

(12) LIFTON, R. 1964. The Woman in America. Beacon Press, Boston.

(13) MILLET, K. 1970. Sexual Politics. Doubleday, Garden City, N. Y.

(14) MOYNIHAN, D. 1967. A family policy for the nation. *In* The Moynihan Report and the Politics of Controversy, L. Rainwater and W. Yancey, eds. M.I.T. Press, Cambridge.

(15) NYE, I. and HOFFMAN, L. 1963. The Employed Mother in America. Rand-McNally, Chicago.

(16) OGBURN, W. and NIMKOFF, M. 1953. Technology and the Changing Family. Houghton-Mifflin, Boston.

(17) PARSONS, T. and BALES, R. 1955. Family, Socialization, and Interaction Process. The Free Press, Glencoe, Ill.

(18) REISS, I. 1969. Premarital sexual standards, *In* The Individual, Sex and Society, C. Broderick and J. Bernard, eds. Johns Hopkins Press, Baltimore.

(19) SEELEY, J., SIM, R. and LOOSLEY, E. 1956. Crestwood Heights. Wiley (Science Editions, 1963), New York.

(20) SIMON, K. and GRANT, W. 1969. Digest of Educational Statistics. U. S. Department of Health, Education and Welfare. U. S. Government Printing Office, Washington, D. C.

(21) SMUTS, R. 1959. Women and Work in America. Columbia University Press, New York.

(22) THOMASSON, R. 1966. Why has American fertility been so high? *In* Kinship and Family Organization. B. Farber, ed. Wiley, New York.

(23) U. S. DEPARTMENT OF LABOR, BUREAU OF LABOR STATISTICS. 1969. Handbook of Labor Statistics, Bulletin no. 1630.

(24) U. S. WOMEN'S BUREAU. 1969. Handbook of Women Workers. Bulletin 294.

(25) U. S. WOMEN'S BUREAU. 1969. Trends in Educational Attainment.

(26) U. S. WOMEN'S BUREAU. 1947. Women's Occupations Through Seven Decades. Bulletin 218.

(27) VADAKIN, J. 1958. Family Allowances: An Analysis of Their Development and Implications. University of Miami Press, Miami.

(28) VADAKIN, J. 1968. Children, Poverty and Family Allowances. Basic Books, New York.

(29) VAN BORTEL, D. 1954. Homemaking: Concepts, Practices and Attitudes in Two Social Class Groups. Unpublished Ph.D. dissertation, University of Chicago.

(30) WHYTE, W. 1956. The Organization Man. Simon and Schuster, New York.

(31) WOMEN: A JOURNAL OF LIBERATION, INC., 1971. How We Live and With Whom. Winter '71. 3028 Greenmount Ave., Baltimore, Md.

(32) WOOD, F. 1968. Sex and the New Morality. Association Press, New York.

PSYCHOLOGICAL CONSEQUENCES
OF SEXUAL INEQUALITY

Jean Baker Miller
and Ira Mothner

Our current concern with the role of women should lead to major changes in psychiatric theory. Already, the re-examination of women's role has enabled some psychiatrists and psychoanalysts to help a number of women — and even some men — to deal in a new way with feelings of sexual and human inadequacy.

"Re-examination" seems too mild a term for the open conflict likely in the future. For many women, the revolution is at hand. Yet open conflict, if understood, offers far more productive possibilities for both women and men than the covert conflict it can replace. Is this conflict between the sexes the result of various neuroses and psychoses, or does it represent an existential dilemma, unrelated to time and place — the inevitability of the two sexes misunderstanding and thwarting each other?

Before one can settle on either of these explanations, one should examine the implications of another proposition, more obvious yet strangely neglected. In our society there exists a thoroughly realistic basis for conflict: men and women are irrationally defined as unequal. It is striking that, in a field that attempts to define, differentiate, and promulgate rationality, so few psychiatrists have studied or even recognized the irrationalities with which we all live. Understanding the conflict between men and women requires some exploration of the psychological consequences of irrational inequality.

All relationships that are irrationally unequal (*e.g.* blacks and whites, women and men) share characteristics that lead to profound psychological results. Many of these seem obvious. Yet, we rarely acknowledge them when dealing with situations that are, in fact, caused by characteristics as apparent as these:

1. Both parties are tied to each other in many ways and affect each other profoundly. Indeed, they need each other.

2. Actions of the dominant group tend to be destructive to the less powerful group. (There are also destructive effects on the dominant group.) All historical experience confirms this tendency.

3. The dominant group usually puts down the less powerful group, labeling it defective in various ways ("blacks are less intelligent than whites," "women are ruled by emotion"). This derogation can take many subtle forms, even seeming to elevate the subordinate. Artists and intellectuals attempt to find all truth in the soul of the black, or the secret of life in the womb of the woman; any soul or womb will do, and thus they deny the individuality of the black or the woman.

4. The dominant group usually acts to halt any movement towards equality by the subordinate group. It also militates strongly against stirrings of rationality or greater humanity in any of its own members. (It was not too long ago that "nigger lover" was a common appellation, and men who let their women have more than the usual rights are still subject to ridicule in many circles.)

5. The dominant group obscures the true nature of the relationship, that is, the very fact of the existence of inequality itself. It rationalizes the situation by other, always false explanations, such as racial or sexual inferiority. This point has particular application to psychoanalytic theory, which, despite overwhelming evidence to the contrary, is still rooted in the notion that women are meant to be passive, submissive, and docile — in short, secondary. From this premise the outcome of therapy is often determined.

6. By proffering one or more "acceptable" roles, the dominants attempt to deny other areas of development to the less powerful. These acceptable roles usually provide a "service" that the dominant group does not choose to, or cannot, do for itself. The functions that the dominant group prefers to perform are closely guarded and closed off

to the subordinates. The ability of subordinates to perform other roles is usually manifest only in emergency situations such as war-time, when inexperienced and untrained blacks and "incompetent" women suddenly "man" the factories with great skill.

7. Since the dominants determine society's ethos, its philosophy, morality, social theory, and its science, they legitimatize the unequal relationship and incorporate it into all of society's guiding cultural concepts.

8. The dominant group is the model for "normal human relationships." Thus, it may then be "normal" to treat others destructively and derogate them, obscure the truth of what you are doing, create false explanations for it, and oppose actions toward equality.

9. The dominant group, then, is bound to suppress disruption of these relationships and to avoid open conflict that might bring into question the validity of the established situation.

Certainly, the dominant group is setting the stage for conflict with the subordinates; and yet it insists there is no cause for conflict. Its interests are being served by the unequal relationship (clearly oppressive to the less powerful group) but its rationalization of that relationship is so well integrated that the dominants actually come to believe that both groups share the same interests.

The dominants' faith in the *rightness* of the relationship is nowhere more apparent than in their attempts to impose that relationship where it does not exist or does not exist as rigidly as seems proper to them. The great distress of white, male social theorists with matriarchal, black families would seem evidence of this.

Since the dominants have determined what is "normal" for society, and their ethos prevails, we are not very familiar with how subordinates deal with their part of the relationship. Because the less powerful group is discouraged from free expression and action, we are only now learning about their experience, thoughts and feelings. The first such expression always comes as a surprise to the dominants, and is usually rejected as strangely atypical. After all, the dominants *knew* that blacks were always happy and cheerful, albeit lazy and shiftless, and that all women really want and need is a man at the center of their lives. What they don't understand is what "they," the first to speak out, are so angry about.

The subordinate group is initially less able to buck the line than the dominants are to hold it. The characteristics that typify their part in the relationship are even more complex:

1. The less powerful group is primarily concerned with its survival. Accordingly, direct, honest reactions to destructive treatment are avoided. Open action in their own self-interest can (and in some places still does) literally result in death. For women in our society this kind of action may mean economic hardship, social ostracism, psychological isolation and even the diagnosis of personality disorder by some psychiatrists.

2. The underpowered group then resorts to various disguised reactions, to "put on" the oppressor while appearing to please him. Black stories, Jewish stories, and various folk tales are full of such humorous examples. In that sense, the "mother knows best" school of literature (*e.g.*, Herman Wouk) and the television family comedies in which father is absurdly manipulated by mother, seem almost the continuation of such folk "wisdom."

3. The less powerful may absorb some of the untruths created by the dominants, so that there are blacks who feel inferior and women who believe they are less important than men. This is more likely to occur if there are few or no alternate concepts at hand. In the short period since the women's movement began, many women in therapy are beginning to raise the issue of their own needs and interests. Previously they would have felt no right to define an issue in this way, rushing on, instead, to question what is wrong with them that makes them unable to fit into their husband's needs and plans.

4. Members of the subordinate group also have experiences and perceptions that more accurately reflect the truth about themselves and the irrationality of their positions. Their own more truthful conceptions are bound to come into opposition with the mythology they have absorbed from the dominant group. An inner tension between these two sets of concepts and their derivatives is almost inevitable.

5. Despite the obstacles, the subordinate group always tends to move towards free expression and action. There were always some slaves who revolted; there were some women who spoke out. Most records of these actions are not preserved by the dominant culture, thus making it difficult for the subordinate group to find a supporting tradition and history.

6. Within each subordinate group there is a tendency for some members to imitate the dominants and to treat their fellow subordinates just as destructively. Psychologists have described this as "identification with the aggressor." Others may attempt to reverse the roles of oppressor and oppressed. Being a subordinate in one relationship does

not necessarily guarantee a benign effect upon one's performance as a dominant in another relationship. (Blacks may put down women; workers may put down blacks and women.)

7. To the extent that the subordinates move toward free expression, exposing the inequality and questioning the basis for its existence, they create open conflict.

What is immediately apparent from the characteristics of these two groups is that mutually enhancing interaction is not probable between unequals. The dominant group is denied direct, honest reaction to its actions, consensual validation or feedback. With no wholly truthful reactions to guide them, the dominants go on dispensing all knowledge and wisdom for society, building distortions on top of distortions.

The characteristics common to all unequal relationships take on special impact in the case of the man-woman relationship. Each needs to develop individually and also needs growing and intimate affection, satisfaction and affirmation from the other. In intimate human relationships if growth does not occur, deterioration of the relationship and of each person ensues. Things rarely stand still.

Before today, women often pressed for validation of their importance without full awareness of why it was denied them. The facts of denial were plain enough: they were not encouraged, often not allowed, to develop their full capacities; they were told their development was less important and should not interfere with men's development; they were, in short, held less important, less valued, less valuable.

As a result, their search for development and participation in a useful and meaningful life assumed special proportions. Women tended to load their ambitions upon husbands and children. Most women felt valued only if they could win favor in the eyes of men, and useful only if their children repeatedly demonstrated to them that they were so. Clearly, women have desires and capacities that cannot be contained within these narrow boundaries.

It was perfectly apparent to anyone able to observe the psychological problems of men and women that women were struggling against the bonds of inequality, engaging in conflict and using heavy weapons. Their campaign, however, was covert. It had no useful objectives, was aimed at no real enemy, was waged with no plan, no order. Indeed, there was no real recognition by many of the combatants that the battle was underway. They fought secretly, and, in most instances, uncomprehendingly. And the battle field was most often their own families.

Within many homes in which the woman seemed to accept her place as subordinate, one variant or another of the following scenario unfolded. The wife would complain of or even merely mention the family's lacks, the limitations of their budget, the possessions they did not have. She made clear, perhaps without even verbalizing it, her feelings that her husband was less able, less successful, less adequate than other men. She constantly demonstrated his relative unimportance within the home and indicated that his failure to find sufficient time for his family was the result of his own inefficiency. Meanwhile, she flaunted her own qualities as a worker, dramatizing the speed and efficiency with which she cared for the home. She, of course, spent much more time with the family and used the time to demonstrate her greater devotion and "love." She capitalized upon whatever weaknesses her husband possessed. He tended, for example, to make impulsive decisions which he, himself, sometimes regretted. He could never admit this, because his wife magnified these errors, falsely creating the impression that they were the cause of many of the family's problems. By contrasting her own more sober reflections she attempted to establish her superiority. Her husband was unable to defend himself against much of this psychological sabotage. Each charge contained some truth. In family discussions, the wife used his weaknesses to humiliate him and treat him with contempt. In time, he came to feel increasingly inadequate, less successful, less "manly," humiliated and demeaned. His children then regarded him as weak, less masterful and mature than their mother. They turned increasingly to mother for fulfillment of their needs, and simultaneiously hated and distrusted her for the destruction of their father.

The wife had waged a devastatingly effective covert campaign, destroying the nominal enemy but gaining no victory. Her husband's effectiveness had been diminished both within the home and outside it. The wife, however, had won nothing. She could not replace the husband she had rendered impotent. She was truly afraid to go out into the world and accomplish anything herself. Indeed, she was ill-prepared to do so, having earlier surrendered her opportunities for education or work experience in order to advance her husband's. During the course of the campaign, she had also lost much and was made to feel unappreciated as a person and less of a woman.

This woman was not asking for equality. She was not struggling to develop her capacities or interests. If she had been, she undoubtedly would have run into conflict with her husband — but conflict of a very different nature.

There are numerous variations of the theme, some even more subtle. In working class families similar processes operate, but the husband may appear more dominant and the wife be more restricted in her words and movements. A tyrannical truck driver's recent remark reflected the fact that he harbors an inner feeling that he is not valued, that he and his wife constantly drain rather than augment each other: "No matter what I do, I know she still thinks I'm a jerk."

Such covert conflict tends to have certain constant characteristics. There is no real resolution or satisfaction possible. The "winner" gains little beyond resentment and the withdrawal of affection. Neither party perceives or learns anything new. Neither is helped towards a new basis for action. The distortions of each are usually reinforced and defended even more strongly. This leads not just to a repetition of the same, but to a progressive deterioration of the personalities of each party and of the relationship between them.

The process of the conflict itself has a fairly regular quality. There is usually an attempt to foreclose the outcome, guarantee the result, insure victory. One tries to avoid a true clash of interest by aiming instead for the psychological destruction of the opponent. It is very easy to undercut, diminish and eliminate the effectiveness of a mate. Any woman, who knows a man, can convey the notion that he is not very much of one. Meanwhile, the real objectives, the factors that create the unequal relationship, are never attacked. The old model of repression remains unchanged, except that the goal of some women has become the reversal of the roles of oppressor and oppressed.

Overt conflict is far more demanding. It takes courage and strength. It involves risk, and women don't have much to fall back on should they lose. The process here is different. Desires are openly stated, and opponents are invited to respond with equal openness and honesty. Although the subordinates in this relationship may have little hope that the male dominants will fight fairly, they keep their own tactics clear. The subordinates engage an opponent who is armed with all of his psychological assets. They do not attempt to deprive him of his psychological resources as an alternative to true conflict over the real issues. The goal is equality and integrity for each, not the destruction of either.

Open conflict offers a chance for resolution. Women, the subordinates, stand to gain their freedom. Men can enjoy the benefits of a more equal relationship, although they may have to admit to old wrongs and reexamine old values. But this is change, not defeat, and growth can occur for both men and women, producing new satisfactions and new ways of valuing each other. The result then includes at least the possibility of new development for each party. Each may perceive some of what the other is trying to express and may be able to utilize this new knowledge to formulate new action. The new action is not forced, but a choice based on new information.

However, when dominants first perceive within the ranks of the less powerful, the beginnings of overt conflict, they almost always confuse what they are seeing with the more destructive model, the covert conflict they have never recognized as any kind of conflict at all. These two models of conflict are easily confused. In psychiatriatric practice, one can readily observe this. There is often a shift from one model to the other without any realization of this by the participants. The dominants feel threatened, even though open action for equality is not aimed at their destruction. It is a challenge to change. While this change might free the dominants from the psychological assaults of covert conflict and offer them an opportunity for new satisfaction, it would also destroy their dominant role. It is a threat not to their persons or their psyches, but to their position of privilege.

Unfortunately, the dominants usually fail to count the true cost of their dominance. They do not know the new satisfaction equality can bring. Indeed, they are unaware of what the denial of truthful feedback has already cost them. Losing out on positive reactions, as well as negative ones, has deprived them of pleasure as well as reality.

As we come to better understand the extent to which characteristics of irrational inequality have snarled relationships between races, sexes, and generations, we can only breathe a collective sigh of relief that the conflicts are now coming into the open. With what we know about the damage of covert conflict, it seems no accident that the "cause" of one psychological problem after another was "discovered" during the period immediately preceding the current women's movement to be the dominant mother and the weak, ineffectual and emotionally removed father. This was held to be true for schizophrenia, homosexuality, alienation and a number of other personality disorders.

The dominant mother-ineffectual father theme also pervaded fiction and drama (*e.g.*, Philip Roth, Edward Albee, *et al*). There is more than a hint here of how important the women's movement may be for psychological theory. When more than half the nation is fighting to establish its sense of self-value, and the other half is defending, with untruths, its irrational dominance, and all of this is going on in disguised and confused ways, there would seem a basis for much of what we now consider "functional psychological disturbance." The serious disturbance of children from families that have been ravaged by this kind of conflict are not simply idiosyncratic occurrences but intensified examples of a situation that exists for all.

Though this formulation of the "dominant mother-ineffectual father" as the cause of practically every serious psychological difficulty was an incomplete description of the situation, it probably did reflect observations that occurred with some degree of regularity. The underlying inequality that leads to such situations was never examined or even recognized. More sophisticated psychiatrists (*e.g.*, Theodore Lidz) have already moved on to more complex delineations of the total family interactions that provide the seedbed of such disorders. They have already gone beyond the image of the mother as the prime "castrating" yet "sick" cause of all problems. But they still do not include a conception of the family as the arena of the conflicts that arise from the inequity sanctioned by the larger society.

Examining the destructive results of inequality can lead to new theoretical understanding of some of the most serious and perplexing psychological problems. Concealed within the hitherto acceptable status of inequality between men and women are destructive forces with far-reaching ramifications. Precisely because women and men affect each other and their children so intimately and so profoundly, this unequal situation is particularly malignant psychologically and especially difficult to confront squarely. Even some of our most humanitarian psychological theorists seem to accept unquestioningly assumptions based upon it.

The existence of irrational unequal relationships has also caused great problems in other vast areas — those relationships in which there do exist real inequalities: parents and children, teachers and students, doctors and patients, and perhaps therapists and clients. What characterizes these relationships is the understanding that one of the parties presumably possesses qualities which it hopes to impart to the other, e.g., mental or emotional maturity, experience in the world, a body of knowledge or a medical treatment. In marked contrast to situations of irrational inequality, society here decrees that the subordinates are to be helped by the dominants to attain their full stature, full equality.

It is striking that all instances of "rational" inequality constitute dilemmas for our society. Possibly, our lives are so affected by irrational inequalities, we are so busy denying and falsifying them, that we do not know how to deal with those who are truly not equal in certain ways. Our theories on child rearing swing from strict control, which assumes that youngsters have no rights, to the progressive extreme, which grants them absolute equality. Our confusion about inequality in general may be preventing us from finding sound means to help our children grow from unequals to full equals. Certainly the problem of developing identity, independence and authentic autonomy in young people is a central and an unsolved problem in psychology today. We admittedly have no good theory of education. It is likely that these dilemmas are related both to each other and to the fact that we have no idea of how to treat unequals constructively and respectfully. We have no full concept of the process of change from unequal to equal, having experience only with enforcing inequality.

The issue in all these areas is the need of a concept of the process of change from unequal to equal, from lesser to full functioning. Our difficulty with even defining such a process may reflect the fact that we tend to apply the values derived from situations of irrational inequality, including the tendency to suppress *all* conflict. We want children to grow. But when their growth challenges us, we shift rapidly to the tactics of closure and intimidation that characterize our irrationally unequal relationships. We frequently abandon the struggle so necessary for their growth and either shut it off or surrender unconditionally under the delusion that they somehow "know best." We have never learned how to relate to unequals with the goal of ending their inequality.

In a more direct practical way it is apparent that the current women's movement has already helped many women and some men to work on their personal problems more productively. In a short time some women have changed from feeling no sense of self or of worth except as these were defined and valued by a man to a sense of worth based on their own processes of evaluation. Some women have freed themselves from implicit or explicit condemnation of themselves for desires that did not fit into the definition of a person who is supposed to want first and foremost to submit herself to another. The fuller development of outlooks such as these can ultimately lead to relationships with men and children that are freer and more satisfying for all concerned. It is also clear that this process will not proceed easily and smoothly. For each individual there are many complex issues to work out. It will be difficult for all involved and, as always, most difficult for the subordinates, the women.

If change is to come and to extend beyond a small segment of the middle class, it obviously will involve activity in many areas — economic, social, legal, political. Behavioral scientists, however, can play a particularly important role in clarifying the situation. While they may not have created the problem, they have often provided support and rationalization for the existing situation. Their pronouncements carry great weight in current society and filter into the popular media to provide the current "religion" and morality for a large segment of the public. Discussion about women often revolves around what is "normal" or "natural" or "good for mental health." In general, behavioral scientists and practitioners have played a role in rationalizing and sanctifying the status quo publicly, and in enforcing it with their patients either grossly or subtly in their practices. Instead, we can turn to elucidating the destructive effects of inequality, exposing the errors of previous concepts of normality that were based upon it and presenting evidence of the positive advantages gained by people who have struggled for more equal human relationships.

THE SINGLE WOMAN
IN TODAY'S SOCIETY :
A REAPPRAISAL

Margaret Adams

Writing on a theme of major societal significance today — such as the changing role of women — resembles a natural history exercise in which the student starts out to study a particular species, only to find that its ecological status and respondent characteristics have altered beyond recognition. So it is with the topic of single women. This article was planned on the basis of my own life experience as a middle-aged professional single woman, augmented by friends and colleagues of different ages, and reinforced by the model of three maiden aunts who functioned as significant social figures in my English west country childhood. However, considering the subject more carefully, I realized that these seemingly stable and clearly delineated models are to a large extent an anachronistic figment of a by-gone — or at least swiftly passing — social era, and that a fresh definition of what constitutes the single women today must precede any discussion of her social role.

By tradition, the term single has been applied to women who have never been married, and until recently it carried the official, if not de facto, connotation of sexual abstinence. In this way the phenomenon of singleness was the antithesis of marriage, and its clearly defined social status was dependent on marriage being a stable social institution only ruptured by the death of one partner. Today, a different set of variables is needed to identify the single woman category because earlier marriages and easier divorce practices have robbed marriage of its permanence, while easily available and safe contraceptive techniques have made extramarital sex a commonplace. Within this article, then, singleness will apply not only to the numerically restricted group of never-marrieds but will also embrace widows and divorced women who fit other criteria that I am putting forward as the basis for a more relevant concept of singleness by today's social standards.

The primary criterion — or vital prerequisite — of being single is the capacity and opportunity to be economically self-supporting. This basic condition provides the elementary social independence from which most of the other features of singleness derive, and it relates this social status to broader societal issues. Thus the incidence of single women as a defined category within any given society is closely connected with its economic and political system and the roles that devolve on women. A society that engages in periodic bouts of violent warfare will have a surplus of women, so that, unless polygamy is the approved marital pattern, some will be without husbands and have to maintain themselves. In the Middle Ages, for example, lower-class single women found a livelihood on the land, in domestic service, and as alewives or spinners (hence the term spinster) while their upper-class counterparts were absorbed in the religious system as anchorites or nuns.(4) These arrangements came into being to counteract the decimation and absence of the male population occasioned by the Crusades.

A second essential criterion of singleness is social and psychological autonomy. The single woman's basic life-style is emotionally independent of relationships that carry with them long term commitment and a subjugation of personal or individual claims for their maintenance. This means she does not recognize a core relationship with a man as the primary or exclusive source of emotional satisfaction or social identity, neither is she encumbered by direct and statutorily defined dependents such as children. Single women, however, often have to assume some less direct, informal family responsibilities, such as contributing substantially to the financial support of aging, sick, or otherwise needy relatives, taking direct care of them on a temporary or protracted basis, and being available for emotional support and advice at times of crisis. My definition deliberately excludes the many unmarried, divorced, and widowed women who are female heads of families, on the grounds that their situation contains many features not pertinent to the life style of the single woman, and merits a discussion of its own.

The third criterion is a clearly thought through intent to remain single by preference rather than by default of being requested in marriage, either as first venture or following widowhood or divorce. It is important to stress this factor because marriage is invested with such a high premium in American society that very little credence is given to the idea that some women remain unmarried on purpose. Even when the choice seems arbitrarily imposed by a shortage of men, the failure of some personable women to secure a husband may be explained by their selective standards, set so high that they have not been met by the males available. In such cases, it may be inferred that the basic, often unconscious, intention has been realized, though some of these women may be so hitched to the prevailing societal norms as to cherish the belief that they would have liked to have married.

Age is another significant factor and I have selected 30 and upwards as the chronological boundary delimiting the single state, on the grounds that the bulk of unmarried girls in their twenties concentrate their energies on remedying their condition. This assumption is support-ed by statistics(5) of March 1970, which show the following age distribution (in thousands) for single women — 20-24 years, 3012; 25-29 years, 732; 30-34 years, 367; with the three successive decades showing a relatively stable figure between 600 and 660. Thus we see that in the later half of the 20 age group, the number of single women have declined to over a quarter of the figure reported in the 20-24 age group, and that this attenuated number is halved in the next five-year period. On the basis of these figures, one can infer that by 30 most women who are still unmarried are beginning to build up economic independence, an investment in work, and a viable value system that allows them to identify and exploit major sources of personal and social satisfaction in other areas than marriage and family. Even those whose first preference is marriage are compelled to readjust their social sights and relationships because the number of eligible men will have thinned out and their married peers will be caught up in a web of social and domestic activities with which they cannot identify and that do not meet their needs. At this juncture the unmarried woman, if she is not to be plagued by a constant sense of dissatisfaction, must take stock of her situation and carefully evaluate both its negative features and its assets. The remainder of this paper will try to define some of these social issues, and suggest solutions that will enable single women to realize a more viable and socially sanctioned identity.

The problems of unattached women range from the practical

mechanics of day-to-day existence, such as a job and living accommodation, to the more subtle but equally vital questions of social role, acceptability, and personal self-esteem. Most of the intangible difficulties stem from one major core disadvantage, namely that single women constitute a clearly defined minority group that demonstrates a conspicuously deviant pattern of functioning in terms of the dominant value system and the organizational goals of American society. To illustrate: the combined total (in thousands) of single, widowed and divorced women in the age range 30-74 is reported as 11,237 as against 34,826 married women and in what might be termed the age span of greatest social activity, i.e., between 30-54, the unmarried numbered 4,388 in contrast to 25,231 married.(5)

Although the world population crisis is fast turning the nuclear family into an obsolete and negatively redundant system, the myth of the sanctity of family life still has such a tenacious hold on the American imagination that women who eschew this modus vivendi are subject to a subtle array of social sanctions that erode their self-esteem, distort their relationships and disturb their sense of homeostasis in the shifting world scene. Single women, for example, are still the victims of quite outrageous stereotyping in regard to their ascribed characteristics, and their unmarried status is popularly attributed to personal failings, such as lack of sexual attractiveness (whatever that elusive quality may be), unresolved early psychosexual conflicts, narcistic unwillingness to be closely committed to another individual, latent lesbianism. These characteristics may often be present, but if being single was not defined in terms of social deviance they would carry a less pathological connotation.

In this connection it is interesting to note the greater frequency with which psychological reasons have been adduced to explain singleness, rather than equally cogent sociological causes. While women today (except for the very poor and uneducated) have access to an increasingly broad repertoire of interesting opportunities in both work and social spheres, these factors are rarely put forward as serious reasons for not being married; if considered at all they are usually dismissed as second-best sublimated options. We have already mentioned the questionable value of the family as a useful social unit, but no one openly commends the decision of the unattached woman not to ally herself with this dinosaurlike social pattern.

Many of the less flattering qualities traditionally associated with unattached women — rigidity, overpreoccupation with minutiae, lack of self-confidence, excessive diffidence, or the overcompensatory quality of brazen hostility – are invariably attributed to poor ego-functioning, but very little thought is given to the extreme social insecurity within which the single woman has to operate. In a society that grants her sex the semblance of protection and economic support in exchange for subordinate obedience to male supremacy, the single woman who fends for herself is fair game for any exploitation the male-dominated working world chooses to exact. The fact that *all* women are in a relatively powerless position in most significant spheres of life – as demonstrated by salary differentials, sex discrimination in the more prestigious and powerful professional jobs, and numbers of women holding real executive power(1) – means that the single ones have to be highly sensitive to potential exploitation and forearmed with defensive tactics. This social predicament is a more likely reason for aggressive behavior towards men than is the more personal psychological explanation of sexual frustration or defensive denial of forbidden wishes. Furthermore, survival in today's highly competitive society demands a high level of self-assertiveness from both sexes; therefore this characteristic in single women must be seen as part of a societal mode of interaction rather than a personal idiosyncracy of sexual status.

The accusation that single women are malicious or lacking in generosity towards each other also requires a sociological as well as psychological interpretation. The emotional frustration that results from any devalued minority status tends to be turned inwards upon the group, rather than outwards to the social forces responsible: this is the same type of defense mechanism manifested by socially respectable members of racial minorities who castigate the social inadequacy of welfare recipients.

This devalued social definition of single women and the distorted self-image of inferiority that it creates can exert a subtly damaging effect on the quality of social relationships with peers, the opposite sex, and married couples. The insidious conviction of being only second best makes it hard for single women to put a proper value on themselves: they tend to approach relationships in an over-diffident, if not apologetic, frame of mind, and perceive them as bestowing something of value on themselves rather than as of reciprocal benefit. In relationships with men this attitude has been particularly destructive, making women over-susceptible to exploitation and often ending in an abandonment that serves to reinforce the latent conviction of failure.

The more aware single woman, who is becoming liberated from this fettering self-concept of inadequacy, still has some residual uncertainty about her own identity, and in her heterosexual relationships is liable to be caught in a double bind of trying to decide what priority in time and emotional energy to devote to serious involvement with a man, while raising anew the question of how sincerely she is committed to the freedom of being single. For the man in question, there is confusion about the woman's newly emerging identity and the ambiguous and unclear goals of the relationship. The old exploitative options of "getting trapped" or "ditching the girl" no longer seem valid, which evokes anxiety — particularly when it involves redefining the beggar maid in more equitable terms.

Friendships with other single women are prone to a similar kind of problem, particularly if both still believe in the inferior status of women and suspect that each is only using the other's companionship and emotional support as a stopgap to ward off loneliness and fill in the time, pending a more rewarding relationship with a man. Further, the overwhelming importance attached to this latter objective introduces a frustration and desperation heightened by the fear that one may succeed, thus abandoning the other to loneliness and a reinforced sense of underachievement. This ambiguous and destructive situation will improve only when marriage or longterm involvement with the other sex is seen as a matter of personal choice and not of social prestige and obligation.

Relationships with married friends are also invested with hazards, although they offer the best scope for the single woman to be herself, because she is not being measured solely for her sexual viability. She may even lose her poor relation status and be welcomed as someone whose broader range of work experience and more varied social and cultural contacts can introduce a note of novelty into a family situation. To the children, she presents a different facet of the adult world from the familiar one they experience in their own mother and those of their friends. Through this contact the wife is kept aware of roles open to women other than the strictly homemaking one she is momentarily absorbed in; this sort of unobtrusive psychological rein-forcement to the fuller personality and identity of the housebound woman is an important liberating factor. For the husband, the relation-ship with the single friend supplies a fresh dimension to the absorbing model of domesticity with which he and his wife have become saddled, as well as the prospect of other more varied facets of life that both can resume in the future. It also provides opportunity for enjoying additional feminine company in the safe confines of a family friendship.

Here, a comment is needed on the word "safe," which is used deliberately to illustrate another unconscious social and psychological belittlement of the single woman, through its implication of the wife's superior sexual attractiveness, her impregnable sense of security in possession, or implicit reliance on the friend's loyalty. This dilemma of the "friendly threesome," and the underpull of tensions that sustain the relationship, is rarely acknowledged, while almost universal recognition is given to its more pronounced version, the eternal triangle. If she is not careful, the single woman can often unwittingly find herself in the position of being a stand-in spouse, even to being consigned the future care of the husband should he survive his wife. Such situations are reminiscent of Biblical parables, of tribal customs for ensuring the care of dependent survivors, and even suttees — the common factor to all these practices being the testimentary disposition of socially vulnerable women for society's convenience.

I have been concentrating on the more subtle aspects of personal relationships because these are closely tied to the emerging social identity of women and, being less obtrusive, have been overshadowed by more obvious problems. Up till recently, scope for sexual experience presented a major difficulty for single women because of narrow penalizing sexual mores and the actual danger of becoming pregnant. The development of effective and reliable contraceptive techniques that are within women's control has, to a large extent, removed both these obstacles and provided single women with opportunity for sexual relationships equal to those hitherto available to legally married women and *all* men. This end to the double standard of sexual behavior is having an influence on the quality of sexual relationships in that the activity is developing a more strongly social character with less heavy psychological weighting than when it was precarious and taboo. One result seems to be a tendency for sexual liaisons to be more numerous and frequent, with much shorter-term commitment. This is also reflected in the divorce rate,(5) an institutionalized version of the same phenomenon.

In this context I should like to mention the psychological myth that women are more inherently faithful than men in sexual relationships, are inclined to invest more emotion over a longer time span, and feel proportionately traumatized when the relationship terminates. My feeling is that this psychological attribute has been developed over time to rationalize and make bearable a situation into which women were trapped by marriage or recurrent childbearing, and that when these fettering external circumstances open up there will be accompanying internal flexibility and freedom. The freewheeling single woman should be among the first to be emancipated from this misconception and to invest the pejorative term, *promiscuity* (an exclusively female epithet), with the adventurous insouciance evoked by the phrase, *wild oats*. The revelation that women have greater and more sustained capacity for sexual activity than hitherto suspected will add grist to this notion once the prim ideas of monogamous loyalty and irrevocable emotional investment have been exploded.(2,3)

The social relationships of unattached women also present practical difficulties, particularly the question of how to develop a pattern of life that satisfies the need for day-to-day ongoing social intercourse. Apart from a relatively small number of women who have exceptional inner resources of their own or are involved in creative projects that require a good deal of solitary leisure, most single women have to cope with recurrent problems of personal loneliness. To counteract these social lacunae the single woman has to organize a deliberately structured social life for herself and invest a good deal of time and energy in maintaining its momentum.

Establishing a satisfying and stimulating social life bears especially hard on single women when they move to a new community because they have fewer introductory lines of communication than their married counterparts, whose husband and children provide a contact with other families or individuals. Also, as long as single women are regarded as a tiresome surplus, there is a reluctance to co-opt new members of the species into an extant social circle lest they disturb the balance of the sexes. For this same reason, single women are often denied admission to more formal social groups, such as country clubs.

A significant lack in the single woman's life is a congenial, trustworthy, and accessible person to serve as a soundingboard and provide the requisite feedback. To meet this need and to offset potential loneliness many single women are beginning to develop informal, loosely-knit communes of unattached individuals who are not close and intimate friends but operate among each other on the basis of shared needs and reciprocal services. Such a group can provide casual and ad hoc entertainment and an exchange of small but vital homemaking services in times of illness or emergency.

Living accommodation is another problem area for single women, though there has been a substantial development of accommodation suitable for single occupants over the last 40 years. In the 1930s, for example, unmarried professional or white collar women workers frequently had to live at home in the ambiguous role of adult child of the family or in a carefully selected private hotel or woman's residence (often euphemistically termed a "club," as in Muriel Spark's novel, *The Girls of Slender Means*), a bed-sitting room with shared cooking facilities, or, more rarely, a private apartment. Today, efficiency apartments and cooperatives offer a range of independent options. However, the lower salaries earned by women at all levels place an economic bar on their taking advantage of these opportunities (considerable savings are needed to purchase an even modest cooperative) and they are often forced into the compromise of rooming with one or two others in order to meet the rent and maintenance bills. While this may sometimes be a deliberate choice, it is more often an expediency involving a sacrifice of standards — in space or privacy — that diminishes the single woman's social self-sufficiency and autonomy. There is also a subtle prestige factor in that a certain level of social sophistication is associated with having your own menage (vide Helen Gurley Brown!), whereas a household shared by several women has a slightly comic undertone, calling up a residual picture of a college dormitory and adolescence.

Single women are also very vulnerable to harrassment and intimidation by unscrupulous landlords, particularly in areas where there is heavy competition for housing, such as the larger cities to which unattached women tend to migrate because of the greater choice of work and social, educational, and cultural opportunities. Where there is a large financial investment at stake, such as purchasing a house in a socially desirable area, single women are liable to encounter prejudice of the same order experienced by blacks, in which realtors operate on the basis of a preconceived stereotype about the applicant rather than on whether the applicant earns enough money to be an effective purchaser, and to maintain the property at the level demanded by the community. All these problems — major and minor — represent an accumulative discrimination that keeps single women in a chronically second-grade living situation, reduces their social status, and saps their individual and corporate self-respect.

If this has been a rather dismal catalogue of complaints about the social condition of single women, I want to end with a brief account of what I consider to be some of the invaluable assets that also attach to this status. My intent in delineating the disadvantages has been to help identify the negative social forces that stand in the way of these assets being fully realized. By making explicit the severe psychological and social devaluation that has settled like an accretion around the concept of singleness, I mean to imply that this attitude is a societal product capable of being changed once its destructive potential is understood. By pointing up the practical difficulties single women face in every day living, I hope to set in motion ingenious ideas and innovative experiments that will develop more efficient social arrangements to minimize these hazards.

The advantages of being single are two-fold — those that redound directly upon the single woman and those that accrue to the corporate good of society. To start with individual benefits, the unmarried woman has greater freedom to take advantage of the exceptional opportunities for new experiences offered by today's rapidly changing world. This can mean moving to work in a different city, country, or continent; it can mean leaving one type of employment for another. For the well-paid professional woman who has been able to save, this freedom from personal commitment allows her to purchase time and involve herself in some different creative activity such as traveling, writing a book, or continuing her education. Because her psychic energy is not primarily invested in the emotionally absorbing task of maintaining a home, a family, or a partner whose needs have to take precedence, the single woman can be more receptive to fresh experience and new ideas, and is able to develop the heightened capacity for social analysis and commentary so vital in today's swiftly evolving pre-revolutionary society. She also has greater freedom to involve herself in social action and reform movements, including activities that involve a high degree of risk-taking, such as being fired from employment, arrested for civil disobedience or physically assaulted by today's violently repressive process of law and order.

Having examined the social entity of the single woman and the debits and assets of the role she has been alloted in today's society, we must now consider how her societal characteristics relate to the radical women's movement, whether she has a special contribution to make to this dynamic social trend, and what impact its changes will have upon her modus vivendi.

The radical feminist movement has three major goals. First, to help women free themselves from the socially restrictive and psychologically enervating roles into which they have been forced by the exigencies of a male-dominated social system. Second, to demonstrate the connection between the tyranny imposed upon women as a sex and the exploitation of all powerless groups, both of which are an inevitable outcome of a capitalist economy. Third, to tap and channel the constructive social energy of women — currently dissipated in many futile, if not destructive, activities — as a motive force for propelling the basic social changes needed to bring about a more equitable and functional distribution of power.

In brief, the aim of women's liberation is to change the prevailing ideas about women — their rights, their potentialities, their aspirations; to change the social structure that has created and still supports this impotent definition; and to offer women, along with other oppressed groups, the opportunity to assume a more viable and satisfying social role with corresponding different functions and life styles.

How does the single woman fit into this scheme? Two areas immediately suggest themselves: psychological emancipation, and radical redefinition with altered social status and functioning.

The single woman, as we have seen, has been a particular victim of the psychological enslavement to which all women have been subjected. Feminist writing has frequently focused on the plight of married women, emphasizing the psychological seduction that has enmeshed them in the spider-web belief that their domesticated condition represents physical, mental, and cultural fulfillment. Less is said about the other side of the coin by which those outside of marriage are saddled with a sense of deprivation, deficit, and alienation. By defining women as sound, whole, viable beings in their own right the radical movement has restored the single woman's sense of self-esteem and put her into the mainstream of social acceptability and importance. Single women, if they can recognize the assets attaching to their status, are in a position to offer a more sharply defined model for the emerging societal roles that may devolve upon women.

Because of the stringent necessity to be economically self-supporting, single women have also had to develop a greater sense of personal independence and some practical expertise in fending for themselves in a discriminating economic sphere. Women in the working and professional world have been conspicuously lacking in executive power, but involvement in this masculine arena, even at a lower social level, has given them an intimate familiarity with the habits of the male and the ecology of his power system. Such knowledge can be turned to good diagnostic account when the time comes for invading that system and instituting radical change. This knowledge is shared by all the female work force but the greater investment that single women are likely to have in their work, which is not only their economic mainstay but also a major force in defining their social identity, probably gives them sharper insights. The business executive's indefatigable secretary, the loyal nurse-receptionist who is privy to her doctor-employer's professional commitments, the woman faculty member, if they do not have a domestic male figure on which to exercise these observational skills, become very adept at sizing up the quirks, weaknesses, strengths and Achilles' heels of their male colleagues, much as potential revolutionaries study the characteristics of the regime they plan to overthrow. What may start as an intuitive diversion becomes a self-conscious exercise with important educational significance.

In terms of purposeful intent, single women are also likely to have a greater capacity for hardheaded, clear-thinking judgment because they are not influenced by the same conflicts and ambivalences that necessarily afflict women who are in a relationship of affectionate amity with a husband or longterm equivalent. This is not to say that the radical feminist movement is the work of single women alone, since the facts suggest quite the opposite, but merely that some of the burdens fall more heavily on their married counterparts.

Finally, what effect will radical change have on the small coterie of women I have designated as single? First, they are likely to be rendered obsolete as a specifically defined group, and far from being in a deviant minority may find that their situation has been transformed into the popular norm. This corresponds with the position that is currently predicted and advocated by many radical feminist writers. The threat of overpopulation and diminishing food supply has already begun to rob marriage of its vital rationale — *i.e.*, the procreation of children and maintenance of a stable family setting for their nurturance — and as more attention is focused on the importance of restricting population growth, marriage will come to be seen as a societal liability perpetuating an outmoded dysfunctional social system. Once women become disabused of the notion that marriage and rearing a family represent the most rewarding way of life, and can choose the sort of life they want to lead and where to invest their social energies and skills, there will be a much smaller drift toward this goal. I arbitrarily imposed the lower age limit of 30 on my definition of singleness to highlight its antithetical stance to marriage; when the lure of the latter has receded, singleness may become the more widely sought option and some of the characteristics and interactive patterns that I have described as pertaining to the present day single woman may be assumed by women in the younger age bracket.

What effect this change of focus will have on women's social objectives and opportunities remains to be seen, but we can speculate that there will be greater and more visible scope for individuals to develop what Ruth Benedict terms their "congenial responses" instead of the contorted antics pre-ordained by society. Those for whom pursuit of knowledge, exploration of ideas, and wider range of experience have a greater appeal than do close interpersonal relationships will be freer to follow this bent without having to pay lip service to the other, more socially dominating, objective of securing a lifelong male companion. Others for whom emotional involvement has higher priority will be able to rechannel their nurturing and protective impulses into public activities that foster the common weal rather than the private family unit. The diminished few who mate and produce children will be the minority, and their pattern of life will approximate more to that of their working counterparts who are unencumbered by dependents. Day care and other socially contrived family supports will be essential pieces of equipment for child-rearing, as the vacuum cleaner is for housework, and mothers — with or without attendant spouses — will be expected and encouraged to develop a wider sphere of interest than the narrow unit of the family within which most of them are currently confined. This trend has already been set in motion. When it attains its full momentum the more obvious differences between the officially single and officially married woman will be absorbed in a new common life pattern.

References

(1) HEDGES, J. 1970. Women workers and manpower demands in the 1970s. *In* Women at Work: Monthly Labor Review. U. S. Dept. of Labor, Bureau of Labor Statistics. Government Printing Office, Washington, D. C.

(2) MASTERS, W. and JOHNSON, V. 1966. Human Sexual Response. Little, Brown, Boston.

(3) MASTERS, W. and JOHNSON, V. 1970. Human Sexual Inadequacy. Little, Brown, Boston.

(4) POWER, E. 1926. The position of women. *In* The Legacy of the Middle Ages, C. Crump and E. Jacob, eds. Clarendon Press, Oxford.

(5) U. S. DEPT. OF COMMERCE. 1971. Statistical Abstracts of the United States. Government Printing Office, Washington, D. C.

RECENT WRITINGS
OF THE WOMEN'S MOVEMENT

Tomannie T. Walker
Catherine Kohler Riessman

The Black Woman

In the last decade, the "invisible man" — the American black — became visible, articulate, and, at last, demanding. Gathering momentum as it grew, strong and vital in spite of the assassinations of its leaders, the Black Revolution in America is today militant, angry, aggressive, and effective. As tactics changed from wrestling legal rights through court action to freedom rides and sit-ins to economic boycotts to open rage expressed in riots and rebellion, as organizational leadership went from NAACP to SCLC to Black Panthers, the facets of American racism have been exposed and subjected to continual effective attack.

Concurrent with aggressive action, and forming the strong base for identifying racism in all its social disguises, is the growth of a theoretical groundwork for understanding the history and development of racism: its economic genesis, its hydra-headed growth, and its perpetuation by subtle, insidious traditions. Clearly these traditions were devised to render the black victim helpless and hopeless, a collaborator in his own agony. The basic institutions of the society —

religious, educational, cultural, legal — have not only been distorted and misshapen by American racism, but, most revealingly, white society has complacently perceived these monstrous distortions as normal, usual, and ordinary.

Because of the way in which racism is interwoven through the whole fabric of society, the process of understanding and identifying its manifestations, in order that they may be attacked and destroyed, has been one of painstaking evaluation. The evaluations and searchings thus generated have now exploded into print in articles, books, poems, plays, and novels made readily and inexpensively available by paperback publishers.

One of the most graphic of these paperbacks is *The Black Woman,* edited by Toni Cade (New York: New American Library. 1970. $0.95. Paperbound). It is a collection of poems, short stories, essays, speeches, and round-table discussions by black women on their position and condition in contemporary American society. It is an important book because it does not confine itself to pathos and poignancy. The poems by Nikki Giovanni, Kay Lindsay, and Audre Lorde, as well as the stories of Paule Marshall and Shirley Williams, vividly and effectively communicate the feelings of black women forced into the most degraded position in American society. These pieces make evident the need for the essays that follow, which evaluate the factors in the oppression of black women, and weigh methods of destroying the racist elements that divest them of dignity, worth, respect and — most vitally — self-respect.

Two subjects heretofore seldom seen in print are contained in essays in this book: the relationship of black women to black men, and the relationship of black women to the women's liberation movement. These areas of thought are intertwined in many of the essays and are discussed from a number of diverse angles. The editor's own articles, "On the Issue of Roles" and "The Pill: Genocide or Liberation," explore this little-understood relationship of black male and female. She scores the tendency, apparent in some militant organizations, of black men to seek the manhood stolen from them for generations in America, by oppressing and exploiting black women. She exposes the roots of the oppression of all black people and makes clear the generative tie between white oppression and black male oppression of black women. She says, "Perhaps we need to let go of all notions of manhood and femininity and concentrate on Blackhood."

In this context, the response of black women to the women's

liberation movement is examined and clarified. The struggle of black women to achieve status and dignity is rightfully seen as an integral part of the total black liberation movement. In "Motherhood," an article by Joanna Clark, sharp satire delineates the indignities to which black women are subjected daily, including those existing in marriage to a black man emasculated by American racism. The skillful writing, often underlined by shock or humor, makes the reader startlingly aware of the social oppression extant in daily living.

Many of the articles are by angry young women willing to face and evaluate harsh facts. Their forthrightness makes it impossible to side-step or hide self-deceptively from a clear look at the actual condition of life for black women. The issues are sharply focused and help the reader to see beyond the limitations of the racist-produced blinders that circumscribe her vision, understanding, and life. This book stimulates thinking, motivates self-re-examination, and generates vital new ideas that both reflect the preoccupations of today's black women and project the issues relevant and contributory to tomorrow's understanding and action.

$-$ T. T. W.

Sisterhood Is Powerful

Sisterhood is Powerful: An Anthology of Writings from the Women's Liberation Movement (New York: Vintage Books. 1970. 602 pp. $2.45.) is one of numerous recent books on women. It was chosen to be reviewed because of the range of opinions it encompasses; the wide spectrum of the current women's movement is represented, and thus offers the reader ready access to the many issues and often conflicting points of view characteristic of this movement today. The editor, Robin Morgan, is an activist in the movement. She does not pretend to be a scholar, indeed, she appears to have little patience for logical, systematic thought ("there is a certain kind of linear, tight, dry, boring, male super-consistency that we are beginning to reject"). The first line of her introduction reveals her bias: "this book is an action." The aim is toward personal and political change, rather than on "objectively" observing the phenomenon of the role of women in our society. Thus, some of the articles are blindly partisan, personal, and urgent in their appeal for change. This is not necessarily to disparage them; on the contrary, it is more often from the personal, experiential and immediate concerns that political movements are made, and that new areas of inquiry are opened up. Clearly the women's movement of today has raised some crucial questions, too long neglected by the scholarly, which we must now begin to examine systematically.

The anthology attempts to encompass the full range of women's views about women. The reader is offered a smorgasbord, as it were, including some thoughtful, well researched, and rational pieces. Included also are several pieces in which gross pathology, distortion and manipulation of fact are masked as politically radical, *e.g.* in excerpts from SCUM (Society For Cutting Up Men) Manifesto: "Scum will couple-bust-barge into mixed (male-female) couples, wherever they are, and bust them up . . . The few remaining men can exist out their puny days . . . or can go off to the nearest friendly suicide center where they will be quietly, quickly and painlessly gassed to death." However, these are the excesses of a transitional period; they do not characterize the movement as a whole, and should not deter a serious reading of the anthology. One does not judge a movement by its excesses, unless one is out to demean it.

Of the seventy-odd pieces that comprise the anthology several are reprinted from other sources, ranging from "respectable," scientific journals to "new left" and women's liberation publications, such as RAT. Most of the pieces, however, were written especially for the anthology, many by authors who are well known in other areas: attorneys Eleanor Holmes Norton and Florynce Kennedy; writer and controversial professor Mary Daly; Lt. Susan Shnall, court-martialled for war resistance. Other authors are not well known, but are qualified as contributors by their personal experiences as talented women unable to advance in our society. The articles are all from the present period, and it is only in the excellent historical article by Brown and Seitz (ironically titled "You've Come a Long Way Baby") that the reader is exposed to the work of earlier writers on the subject, including Thomas Paine, Sarah Bagley, and Frances Trollope.

From the viewpoint of the sociology of knowledge, one must ask: why such a movement now? What political and social forces have led to a resurgence of a new kind of feminist movement and a literature to substantiate it?

The black revolution of the 60s clearly stimulated other groups in society to examine and fight paternalism and discrimination foisted on them: Puerto Ricans, Chicanos, students and women. Brown and Seitz note that, similarly, the abolitionist movement of the 1840s gave birth to the official beginning of the women's rights movement in the United States. Those who question the status quo apparently stimulate processes (group contagion), become role models, and in other ways set the ground work for other groups to attempt to change the social order. Even in the imagery and rhetoric of the current women's movement, imitative qualities are apparent: "liberation," "oppression," "sexism" (from racism), and the like.

Morgan cites experience in the civil rights struggle and in New Left organizations as a propelling force in the development of the women's rights movement.

> Thinking we were involved in the struggle to build a new society, it was a slowly dawning and depressing realization that we were doing the same work and playing the same roles *in* the movement as out of it: typing the speeches that men delivered, making coffee but not policy, being accessories to the men whose politics would supposedly replace the Old Order.

Anger at this experience led some women to write position papers, form caucuses, and eventually split off and form their own organizations.

It is interesting to note that in this present period, characterized by a reduction in activism by blacks and youth, the equalitarian struggle of women should achieve such prominence. Perhaps this movement is the least threatening to the larger social order; it is seen as revolution-at-home, or in the demi-institutions of the society.

The anthology amply documents the pervasive and often insidious ways in which women are prevented equal access in society. Diane B. Schulder surveys criminal and welfare law, and statutes that prevent women from holding property and entering into legal contracts. Her point is that sex discrimination exists in the very definition of crimes (e.g., adultery, prostitution) and that prejudice is "enshrined in laws." Other articles armed with statistics convincingly argue that employment practices are discriminatory, and keep women at the bottom of the economic structure, in positions supplementary to men, not competing with them.

Highly personal accounts by Laura Furman and Lindsy Van Gelder reveal their struggles in gaining entry into publishing and journalism, moving testimony of wasted talent, to say nothing of the pain inflicted by discriminatory practices. The media perpetuate images of the dull normal housewife, or the woman as domestic consumer. It is a subtle, interwoven pattern of oppression which is presented, and Schulder sums up the evasiveness and circular logic: "Laws lead to enforcement of practices. Practices reinforce and lead to prejudice. The cycle continues . . ."

There is a strong section on the mental health profession's contribution to the problem. Susan Lydon and Dr. Mary Jane Sherfey, in separate and very different articles, take issue with many of the myths surrounding female sexuality. Amendations in psychoanalytic theory are called for, based on these new data. Dr. Naomi Weisstein surveys the experimental literature in psychology and shows that what is studied changes radically when there is a change in the social context. The biases and expectations of the examiner, to say nothing of the social expectations, directly influence the results of research studies on sexual differences. Thus, theories of the psychology of women may have evolved that ascribe phenomena to inner traits while ignoring social contexts. Dr. Weisstein succinctly states the issue:

> . . . . it is clear that until social expectations for men and women are equal, until we provide equal respect for both men and women, our answers to this question [are there immutable differences between men and women?] will simply reflect our prejudices.

Psychiatrist Natalie Shainess is critical of the "phallocentric bias" of much of psychoanalytic theory:

> "The great writers have been more perceptive about women, at times, than psychoanalysts, and have understood and accepted woman's drive to be an equal human being. . . . Psychiatrists are urged to examine some of their own prejudices and think more searchingly in interpreting feminine behavior.

The book is strongest in describing what is wrong — where discrimination exists and the subtle ways it is expressed. Where the book falls down is in the area of programmatic reconstruction. Too often the reader is left feeling only a sense of outrage, and the where and how to channel the feelings into constructive action is the missing link. Consciousness is all, seems to be the motto, but no overall strategy for change is offered.

In its frequent overemphasis on the personal, the book contains a fundamental fault of logic: where discrimination exists, it is designed, perpetuated, and encouraged by men; thus, man is the enemy, the "oppressor," to use the rhetoric of the book. As the representative of the power structure, he is the object of woman's rage. The historical and societal forces perpetuating discrimination are thus often discarded in favor of a more personal attack — the shifting, dialectical and interwoven aspects of the pattern are oversimplified. Both logically and tactically, this emphasis appears to be a mistake, although perhaps a common characteristic of political movements. One defines oneself in antithesis to the other, and tends, perhaps needs, to personalize one's rage, to search for an enemy who is concrete, specific, and capable of absorbing one's attack.

The book's most extreme statement is that of Martha Shelley's, "Notes of a Radical Lesbian." "Freedom from oppression by men" is the goal, and thus lesbianism is defined as a *political* act, "one road to freedom." Shelley writes:

> Straight women fear lesbians because we represent an alternative. They fear us for the same reason that uptight middle class people fear hip people. They are angry at us because we have a way out that they are afraid to take.

It is too easy, and essentially inappropriate, to dismiss this point of view as "sick." The issue is posed as a political and social one and must be addressed in these terms (although, interestingly enough, the author herself seeks a mental health rationale for her behavior, e.g., "If hostility to men causes lesbianism, then it seems to me that in a male-dominated society, lesbianism is a sign of mental health.")

The argument for lesbianism rests on the assumption that a relationship between the oppressed cannot be oppressive. Are lesbian relationships, in fact, free of oppression? Is power redistributed? Do these relationships really transcend exploitation and manipulation, or do they frequently duplicate in a new guise the non-equalitarian relationships frequently found between men and women?

Lesbian relationships deny the value of children. Because the tasks of child rearing are difficult, lack social supports, are denied status in our society, and frequently prevent women from self-actualization outside the home, is the ultimate freedom to be free of children?

Lesbianism as a strategy against oppression identifies man as the enemy. Does it not represent a flight from the struggle for equality of the sexes? It is one thing to personalize the problem and direct anger at men; it is quite another to reduce the entire problem to men and interpersonal relationships between men and women.

To make man the enemy, and to glorify sexual unions from which the enemy is excluded, appears to be a poor resolution of the problem for women today. To identify with the male, the aggressor, and to reject and negate those aspects of life for which women are biologically determined, is a mistake. Biology is not everything, but neither is it nothing. Identity (being like) and equality (having equal access and choice) are not the same.

Let it be clear that we are not rejecting lesbianism on mental health grounds, nor because it is culturally "deviant," nor because it is tactically divisive in building broad support for a women's movement. We are rejecting it as a "road to freedom," and as the ultimate political act for women.

What emerges from *Sisterhood is Powerful* is the need for a rethinking of our culture's concepts of "masculinity" and "femininity," and a thorough look at our child rearing patterns to explore the subtle and insidious ways in which myths are propelled and the outcomes programmed. The emotional, personal, and subjective dimensions of the women's movement expressed in this book open new vistas that need to be integrated, absorbed and evaluated scientifically.

— C. K. R.

RESOURCE BIBLIOGRAPHY

Miriam G. Keiffer
Patricia A. Warren

This bibliography is an independent supplement to the proceedings, papers, and discussion sessions of a workshop — The Impact of Fertility Limitation on Women's Life-Career and Personality — sponsored by The New York Academy of Sciences on February 19, 1970. It was compiled in two ways. First, participants in the workshops were requested to submit whatever references they thought should be included. About 70% responded. In addition, bibliographies that were collected by other individuals were consulted.

We are particularly indebted to Lucinda Cisler for the use of her bibliography, which was relied upon not only for references, but also for the beginnings of a cataloging system. Her work, "Women: A Bibliography," is constantly updated and contains many references that go beyond the scope of this bibliography. Requests for the Cisler bibliography (25¢ each, 10 for $2.00, 30 for $5.00) should be sent directly to Lucinda Cisler, 102 W. 80th St., New York, N.Y. 10024. References from this listing are noted by an asterisk in the left margin.

We also are especially grateful to Esther Milner for her help in setting up appropriate categories. Kate Millett and Sandra Tangri were kind enough to permit use of the references from their doctoral dissertations. Also, free use was made of the references in Caroline Bird's "Born Female," Betty Friedan's "The Feminine Mystique," Jessie Bernard's "Academic Women," and the publication list of the Women's Bureau of the Department of Labor. There are probably many more bibliographies that were overlooked, but an attempt was made to incorporate materials on hand.

Users of this bibliography will find references categorized alphabetically under general headings. In some cases, references were listed under two headings when they seemed equally pertinent to both. Some titles were extremely difficult to classify because the subjects of the books were not readily identifiable. We therefore apologize if, on closer examination, a book listed under "economics" really deals with "sexuality," although in the light of current events perhaps that is not such inaccurate categorizing. It is our hope that this bibliography will be a useful tool to both researchers and students in the fields concerned with population limitation and women.

This bibliography is reprinted by permission of the Annals of the New York Academy of Sciences. Copyright © New York Academy of Sciences.

The Changing Family

ACKERMAN, N. 1958. The Psychodynamics of Family Life. New York, N. Y.

*ARIES, P. 1962. *Centuries of Childhood. A Social History of Family Life.* Translated by R. Balick. Random House. New York, N. Y.

*BAGDIKIAN, B. H. 1966. Who is sabotaging day care for our children? Ladies Home J. Nov.:86.

BELL, N. W. & E. F. VOGEL. 1968. A Modern Introduction to the Family. The Free Press. New York, N. Y.

*BENJAMIN, L. 1966. So You Want to be a Working Mother! McGraw-Hill Book Co. New York, N. Y.

*BETTELHEIM, B. 1969. The Children of the Dream: Communal Child-Rearing and American Education. MacMillan Co. New York, N. Y.

BIRD, C. 1967. What we are finding out about working mothers. Women's Day.

*BLOOD, R. O. & D. WOLFE. 1960. Husbands and Wives, the Dynamics of Married Living. The Free Press. Chicago, Ill.

BRIFFAULT, R. 1927. The Mothers: A Study of the Origins of Sentiments and Institutions. (3 vol.) MacMillan. New York, N. Y.

*BRIFFAULT, R. 1959. The Mothers. Allen & Unwin. London, England.

CAIN, G. G. 1966. Married Women in the Labor Force: An Economic Analysis. University of Chicago Press. Chicago, Ill.

*CALHOUN, A. 1935. The Social History of the Family in America.

*COSER, R. 1964. The Family: Its Structure and Functions. St. Martins.

COTTON, D. W. 1965. The Case for the Working Mother. Stein and Day. New York, N. Y.

*DAHLSTROM, E., Ed. 1967. The Changing Roles of Men and Women. Duckworth. London, England.

*ENGELS, F. 1902. The Origins of the Family, Private Property and the State. Translated by E. Untermann. Charles Kerr. Chicago, Ill.

*FELDMAN, H. 1965. Development of the Husband-Wife Relationship. Cornell University Press. Ithaca, N. Y.

FLETCHER, R. 1962. Britain in the Sixties: The Family and Marriage. Penguin. London, England.

*FOLSOM, J. K. 1943. The Family and Democratic Society. John Wiley & Sons, Inc. New York, N. Y.

GEIGER, H. K. 1968. The Family in Soviet Russia. Harvard University Press. Cambridge, Mass.

*GOODE, W. J. 1956. Women in Divorce.

GOODE, W. J. 1964. The Family. Prentice-Hall. Englewood Cliffs, N. J.

*HARTMAN, S. 1969. Should wives work? McCall's. Feb.:57.

JEPHCOTT, P., N. SEEAR & J. H. SMITH. 1962. Married Women Working. Allen & Unwin. London, England.

KALISH, R. A., M. MALONEY & A. ARKOFF. 1966. Cross-cultural comparisons of college student marital-role preferences. J. Soc. Psychol. 68:41−47.

KINGSBURY, S. H. & M. F. FAIRCHILD. 1935. Factory, Family and Women in the Soviet Union. Putnam. New York, N. Y.

KIRKPATRICK, C. 1938. Nazi Germany. Its Women and Family Life. Bobbs-Merrill. Indianapolis, Ind.

*KOMAROVSKY, M. 1964. Blue-Collar Marriage. Random House. New York, N. Y.

*KOOS, E. 1946. Families in Trouble.

MACE, D. & V. MACE. 1963. The Soviet Family. Doubleday. New York, N. Y.

MAKARENKO, A. S. 1967. The Collective Family. Translated by R. Daglish. Doubleday. New York, N. Y.

MEAD, M. 1953. The impact of cultural changes on the family. In: The Family in the Urban Community. D. Tyler, Ed.:3−17. Merrill-Palmer School. Detroit, Mich.

MEAD, M. 1954. Family life is changing. In: Encyclopedia of Child Care and Guidance. S. M. Gruenberg, Ed.: 675−682. Doubleday & Co. Garden City, N. Y.

MEAD, M. 1954. How fares the American family. In: Proceedings of the Annual Convention, Atlantic City, N. J., Official Reports and Records. 58:58−62. National Congress of Parents and Teachers. Chicago, Ill.

MINCER, J. 1962. Labor force participation of married women. In: Aspects of Labor Economics. Princeton University Press. Princeton, N. J.

*MOORE, B. M. & W. H. HOLTZMAN. 1967. Tomorrow's Parents. University of Texas Press. Austin, Tex.

MYRDAL, A. & K. VIOLA. 1956. Women's Two Roles: Home and Work. Routledge and Kegan Paul. London, England.

*NATIONAL MANPOWER COUNCIL. 1957. Womanpower and Work in the Lives of Married Women.

*NYE, F. I. & L. W. HOFFMAN, Eds. 1963. The Employed Mother in America. Rand-McNally, New York, N. Y.

O'NEILL, B. P. 1965. Careers for Women After Marriage and Children. MacMillan Co. New York, N. Y.

*O'NEILL, W. 1967. Divorce in the Progressive Era. Yale University Press. New Haven, Conn.

ORDEN, S. & N. BRADBURN. 1969. Working wives and marriage happiness. Amer. J. Sociol. Jan.

PARSONS, T. & R. BALES. 1955. Family, Socialization and Interaction Process. The Free Press. New York, N. Y.

PETERSON, E. T. 1958. The impact of maternal employment on the mother-daughter relationship and on the daughter's role orientation. Unpublished doctoral dissertation. The University of Michigan. Ann Arbor, Mich.

*PLATO. The communal rearing of children. In: The Republic. Book 5.

*RUDERMAN, F. Child Care and Working Mothers. Child Welfare League of America. New York, N. Y.

*RUSSELL, B. Marriage and Morals. Bantam Press. New York, N. Y.

SCHLESINGER, R. 1949. The Family in the USSR. Routledge. London, England.

*SCHUR, E. M., Ed. 1964. The Family and the Sexual Revolution. University of Indiana. Bloomington, Ind.

SCOFIELD, N. E. 1960. Some changing roles of women in suburbia: A social anthropological case study. Trans. N. Y. Acad. Sci. 22(6).

SOUTHARD, H. F. 1960. July 17. Mothers' dilemma: to work or not? N.Y. Times Mag.

STOLLENWERK, T. 1968. Back to Work. Ladies: A Career Guide for the Mature Woman. Pilot Books. New York, N. Y.

STOLZ, L. M. 1960. Effects of maternal employment on children: Evidence from research. Child Develop. 31(4):749–782.

WOMEN'S BUREAU. 1968. Working mothers and the need for child care services. United States Department of Labor. Wages and Labor Standards Administration. June.

WESTERMARCK, E. 1922. The History of Human Marriage. (5th edit., 3 vol.) MacMillan Co. London, England.

WESTERMARCK, E. 1926. A Short History of Marriage. MacMillan Co. New York, N. Y.

WESTERMARCK, E. 1936. The Future of Marriage in Western Civilization. MacMillan Co. London, England.

WINCH, R. F., R. McGINNINS & H. R. BARRINGER, Eds. 1962. Selected Studies in Marriage and the Family. Holt, Rinehart & Winston. New York, N. Y.

Social and Psychological Influences on Family Size

ADAMS, J. R. 1963. Psycho-social aspects of family limitation and population control: a selected bibliography of English language sources. (Mimeo available from author, Box 199, Teachers College, Columbia University, New York, N. Y. 10027.)

BETANCUR, J. E. & L. GARCIA DE SOUSA. 1959. Current population changes in Latin America and the implications for religious institutions and behavior. Cath. Sociol Rev. Spring.

BHANDARI, L. C. 1957. The psychological aspects of family planning. J. Fam. Welfare. 3:190–194.

*BLAKE, J. 1961. Family Structure in Jamaica: The Social Context of Reproduction.

BLAKE, J. 1967. Income and reproductive motivation. Pop. Stud. 21(3):185–206.

BLAKE, J. 1967. Reproductive ideals and educational attainment among white Americans, 1943–1960. Pop. Stud. Sept.

BLAKE, J. 1968. Are babies consumer durables? Pop. Stud. 22(1):5–25.

*BLOOD, R. O. Long-range causes and consequences of the employment of married women. J. Marr. Fam. 27(1).

BROFENBRENNER, M. & A. BUTTRICK. 1960. Population control in Japan: An economic theory and its application. Law Contemp. Prob. 25(3):536–557.

BUMPASS, L. 1967. Stability and change in family size expectations over the first two years of marriage. J. Soc. Issues 23:83–98.

CALHOUN, J. B. 1962. Population density and social pathology. Sci. Amer. 206:139–148.

CAMPBELL, A. A., P. K. WHELPTON & R. F. TOMASSON. 1961. The reliability of birth expectations of U. S. wives. Int. Pop. Union Conf. Paper No. 70.

CENTERS, R. & G. H. BLUMBERG. 1954. Social and psychological factors in human procreation: A survey approach. J. Soc. Psychol. 40:245–257.

CHRISTENSEN, H. T. 1968. Children in the family: Relationship of number and spacing to marital success. J. Marr. Fam. 30:283–289.

CICOUREL, A. V. 1967. Fertility, family planning, and the social organization of family life: Some methodological issues. J. Soc. Issues 23:57–82.

CLARE, J. E. & C. V. KISER. 1951. Social and psychological factors affecting fertility: XIV. Preference for children of given sex in relation to fertility. Milbank Mem. Fund Quart. 29:440–492.

CLARKSON, F. E., S. R. VOGEL, I. K. BROVERMAN & D. M. BROVERMAN. 1970. Family size and sex role stereotypes. Science 167:390–392.

CLAUSEN, J. A. 1965. Family size and birth order as influences upon socialization and personality: Bibliography and abstracts. Social Science Research Council. New York, N. Y.

COLLVER, O. A. 1968. Women: Work participation and fertility in metropolitan areas. Demography 5:55–60.

CORWIN, A. F. 1963. Contemporary Mexican attitudes toward population, poverty and public opinion. Latin American Monographs, No. 25. University of Florida Press. Gainsville, Fla.

DAVIS, K. 1966. Sociological aspects of genetic control. In: Genetics and the Future of Man. North-Holland Publishing Co. Amsterdam, The Netherlands.

DAVIS, K. & J. BLAKE. 1956. Social structure and fertility: An analytic framework. Econ. Develop. Cultural Change 4:211–235.

DE JONG, G. F. 1965. Religious fundamentalism, socio-economic status, and fertility attitudes in the southern Appalachians. Demography 2:540–548.

DE LESTAPIS, S. 1961. Family Planning and Modern Problems: A Catholic Analysis. Herder & Herder. New York, N. Y.

DEVEREUX, G. A. 1960. A Psychoanalytic Study of Contraception. Planned Parenthood Association. New York, N. Y.

DINITZ, S., R. R. DYNES & A. C. CLARKE. 1954. Preferences for male or female children: Traditional or affectional? Marr. Fam. Living 16:128–130.

ELLIS, A. 1959. Psychological aspects of discouraging contraception. Realist 1:11–13.

FAGLEY, R. M. 1960. The Population Explosion and Christian Responsibility. Oxford University Press. New York, N. Y.

FLANAGAN, J. C. 1942. A study of factors determining family size in a selected professional group. Genet. Psychol. Monogr. 25:3–99.

*FLAGEL, J. C. 1947. Population, Psychology, and Peace. C. A. Watts. London, England.

FREEDMAN, D. S., R. FREEDMAN & P. K. WHELPTON. 1960. Size of family and preference for children of each sex. Amer. J. Sociol. 66:141–146.

FREEDMAN, R. 1963. The Sociology of Human Fertility: A Trend Report and Bibliography. Basil Blackwell. Oxford, England.

FREEDMAN, R. & L. COOMBS. 1966. Childspacing and family economic position. Amer. Sociol. Rev. 31(5):631–648.

FREEDMAN, R. & L. COOMBS. 1966. Economic considerations in family growth decisions. Pop. Stud. 20(2):197–222.

FREEDMAN, R., L. C. COOMBS & L. BUMPASS. 1965. Stability and change in expectations about family size: A longitudinal study. Demography 2:250–275.

GARAI, J. E. 1964. The effect of information on students' knowledge of population problems and their attitudes toward population control Psychology 1(3):15–20.

GARAI, J. E. & A. SCHEINFELD. 1968. Sex differences in mental and behavioral traits. Genet. Psychol. Monogr. 77:199–299.

GIBBONS, W. J. 1956. Fertility control in the light of some recent Catholic statements: I. Eugen. Quart. 3:9–15.

GIBBONS, W. J. 1956. Fertility control in the light of some recent Catholic statements: II. Eugen. Quart. 3:82–87.

GOLDBERG, D., H. SHARP & R. FREEDMAN. 1959. The stability and reliability of expected family size. Milbank Mem. Fund Quart. 37(4):369–385.

GOODE, W. A. 1963. World Revolution and Family Patterns. The Free Press of Glencoe. New York, N. Y.

HAWKES, G. R., L. BURCHINAL & B. GARDNER. 1958. Size of family and adjustment of children. Marr. Fam. Living 20:65.

HILL, R., J. M. STYCOS & K. W. BLACK. 1959. The Family and Population Control: A Puerto Rican Experiment in Social Change. University of North Carolina Press. Chapel Hill, N. C.

HOFFMAN, L. 1968. The decision to become a working wife. In: Family Roles and Interaction: An Anthology, J. Heiss, Ed. Rand-McNally. Chicago, Ill.

HOFFMAN, L. W. & F. WYATT. 1960. Social change and motivations for having larger families: Some theoretical considerations. Merrill-Palmer Quart. 6:235–244.

HOFFMEYER, H. 1953. Social and psychological factors limiting the use of anti-conceptions. Int. J. Sexol. 7:75–76.

HOLLINGWORTH, L. S. 1916. Social devices for compelling women to bear and rear children. Amer. J. Sociol. 22:28–29.

HURLEY, J. R. & D. PALONEN. 1967. Marital satisfaction and child density among university student parents. J. Marr. Fam. 29:483–484.

JAFFE, F. S. 1964. Family planning and poverty. Marr. Family 27:467.

KAHL, J. A. 1967. Modern values and fertility ideals in Brazil and Mexico. J. Soc. Issues 23:99–114.

KELMAN, S. R. 1937. Some psychiatric aspects of birth control. Amer. J. Psychiat. 94:320.

KISER, C. 1968. Trends in fertility differentials by color and socioeconomic status in the United States. Eugen. Quart. 15(4):221–226.

KROGER, W. S. & S. C. FREED. 1951. Psychogynecic aspects of contraception. In: Psychosomatic Gynecology. W. B. Saunders Co. Philadelphia, Pa. Reprinted, 1963. Wilshire. Hollywood, Calif.

LEWIS-FANING, E. 1949. Report on an enquiry into family limitation and its influence on human fertility during the past fifty years. Papers Roy. Commission Population I. Her Majesty's Stationery Office. London, England.

LIEBERMAN, E. J. 1970. Reserving a womb: Case for the small family. Amer. J. Public Health 60(1):87–92.

LIEBERMAN, J. E. 1964. Preventive psychiatry and family planning. J. Marr. Fam. Nov.: 471–477.

LORIMER, F. 1954. Culture and Human Fertility. UNESCO. Paris, France.

MENNINGER, K. 1943. Psychiatric aspects of contraception. Bull. Menninger Clin. 7:36–40.

MISHLER, E. & C. F. WESTOFF. 1955. A proposal for research on social psychological factors affecting fertility: Concepts and hypotheses. Current Research in Human Fertility. Milbank Memorial Fund. New York, N. Y.

NAG, M. 1962. Factors Affecting Fertility in Non-inudstrial Societies. Yale University Publications in Anthropology, No. 66. Yale University Press. New Haven, Conn.

NAMBOODIRI, N. K. 1964. The wife's work experience and child spacing. Milbank Mem. Fund Quart. July:65–77.

NYE, F.I. 1952. Sibling number, broken homes and adjustment. Marr. Fam. Living14:327–330.

POHLMAN, E. 1966. Mobilizing social pressures toward small families. Eugen. Quart. 13(2):122–127.

POHLMAN, E. 1967. A psychologist's introduction to the birth planning literature. J. Soc. Issues 23:13–38.

POHLMAN, E. W. 1966. Birth control: Independent and dependent variable for psychological research. Amer. Psychol. 21:967–970.

POHLMAN, E. W. 1967. The Psychology of Birth Planning. Schenkman. Cambridge, Mass.

POHLMAN, E. & K. S. RAO. 1969. Children, teachers and parents view birth planning, II. Children's family size preferences and their reasons. J. Fam. Welfare 15(3):54–66.

POLGAR, S. 1966. Sociocultural research in family planning in the United States: review and prospects. Human Organization 25:321–329.

POLGAR, S. 1969. Culture and family planning. Paper, Ann. Meet. Soc. Appl. Anthropol. Mexico City, April 10.

RAUF, A. 1958. Psychological aspects of family planning. J. Fam. Welfare 4:85–91.

REED, R. B. 1947. Social and psychological factors affecting fertility: The interrelationship of marital adjustment, fertility control, and size of family. Milbank Mem. Fund Quart. 25:383–425.

REHWINKEL, A. M. 1959. Planned Parenthood and Birth Control in the Light of Christian Ethics. Concordia. St. Louis, Mo.

REGUENA, M. 1965. Social and economic correlates of induced abortion in Santiago, Chile. Demography 2:42.

STYCOS, J. M. 1965. Female employment and fertility in Lima, Peru. Amer. J. Sociol. 70.

SYTCOS, J. M. 1965. Social class and preferred family size in Peru. Amer. J. Sociol. 70:651–658.

STYCOS, J. M. 1967. Contraception and Catholicism in Latin America. J. Soc. Issues 23:115–134.

SULLOWAY, A. W. 1959. Birth Control and Catholic Doctrine. Beacon Press. Boston, Mass.

WESTOFF, C. F., E. G. MISHLER & L. E. KELLY. 1957. Preferences in size of family and eventual fertility twenty years after. Amer. J. Sociol. 62:491–497.

WESTOFF, C. F. & R. H. POTVIN. 1967. College Women and Fertility Values. Princeton University Press. Princeton, N. J.

WHELPTON, P. K. & C. V. KISER, Eds. 1946–1958. Social and Psychological Factors Affecting Fertility. (5 vol.) Milbank Memorial Fund. New York, N. Y.

WYATT, F. 1967. Clinical notes on the motives of reproduction. J. Soc. Issues 23:29–56.

ZIMMERMAN, A. 1961. Catholic Viewpoint and Overpopulation. Hanover House. Garden City, N. Y.

Reproduction Control and Limitation Policy

ADAMS, J. R. 1961. Attitudinal ambivalence and choice of contraceptive method. Unpublished doctoral dissertation. Columbia University. New York, N. Y.

AGARWALA, S. N. 1960. Population control in India: Progress and prospects. Law Contemp. Probl. 25(3):583.

APTEKAR, H. 1931. Anjea: Infanticide Abortion and Contraception in Savage Society. Goodwin. New York, N. Y.

*BANKS, J. A. & O. BANKS. 1954. Prosperity and Parenthood: A Study of Family Planning among the Victorian Middle Classes. Routledge and Kegan Paul. London, England.

*BANKS, J. A. & O. BANKS. 1964. Feminism and Family Planning in Victorian England. Schoken. New York, N. Y.

*BATES, J. E. & E. S. ZAWADSKI. 1964. Criminal Abortion: A Study in Medical Sociology. Charles C. Thomas Publ. Springfield, Ill.

BERELSON, B. & R. FREEDMAN. 1964. A study in fertility control. Sci. Amer. 210:29–37.

BERELSON, B., et al., Eds. 1966. Family Planning and Population Programs. University of Chicago Press. Chicago, Ill.

BLAKE, J. 1965. Demographic science and the redirection of population policy. J. Chron. Dis. 18:1181–1200.

BLAKE, J. 1966. Ideal family size among white Americans: A quarter of a century's evidence. Demography 19.

BLAKE, J. 1967. Family size in the 1960's – a baffling fad? Eugen. Quart. March.

BLAKE, J. 1967. Parental control, delayed marriage, and population policy. Proc. World Population Conf. 1965. II. United Nations. New York, N. Y.

BLAKE, J. 1969. Population policy for Americans. Is the government being misled? Science 164:522–529.

BOGUE, D. J. 1965. Westside fertility report. (Mimeo available from author, Community and Family Study Center, University of Chicago, Chicago, Ill.)

CALDERONE, M. S., Ed. 1958. Abortion in the United States. (Hoeber) Harper & Row. New York, N. Y.

CALDERONE, M. S., Ed. 1964. Manual of Contraceptive Practice. The Williams & Wilkins, Co. Baltimore, Md.

CARLETON, R. O. 1965. Fertility trends, and differentials in Latin America. Milbank Mem. Fund Quart. 43(4):Part 2.

CHANDRASEKHAR, S. 1961. Population and Planned Parenthood in India. 2nd edit. Allen & Unwin. London, England.

CISLER, L. 1970. Abortion law repeal: A warning to women. In: Notes from the Second Year: Radical Feminism. (Reprints available from New Yorkers for Abortion Repeal, P. O. Box 240, Planetarium Station, New York, N. Y. 10024, 15¢ each.)

CISLER, L. 1970. Unfinished business: Birth control and women's liberation. In: The Hand that Cradles the Rock. R. Morgan, Ed. Random House, New York, N. Y. (Reprints available from author, 102 W. 80th St., New York, N. Y. 10024, 25¢ each.)

COLEMAN, R. W., E. KURTS & S. PROVENCE. 1953. The study of variations of early parental attitudes: A preliminary report. Psychoanal. Stud. Child. 8:20–47.

COLLYER, A. O. 1965. Birth Rates in Latin America. Research Series, No. 7. Institute of International Studies. University of California. Berkeley, Calif.

CORNISH, M. J., F. A. RUDERMAN & S. S. SPIVAK. 1963. Doctors and Family Planning. National Committee on Maternal Health. New York, N. Y.

DAVIS, K. 1965. The population impact on children in the world's agrarian countries. Pop. Rev. 9(1&2).

DAY, L. H. & A. T. DAY. 1964. Too Many Americans: Tomorrow's Issue. Houghton-Mifflin. Boston, Mass.

DEVEREUX, C. 1955. A Study of Abortion in Primitive Societies. Julian Press. New York, N. Y.

DICK-READ, G. 1962. Childbirth Without Fear: The Principles and Practices of Natural Childbirth. Dell. New York, N. Y.

DOCTOR X. 1962. Doctor X, the Abortionist. (As told to L. Freeman.) Doubleday. New York, N. Y.

ETZIONI, A. 1968. Sex control, science and society. Science 148:1107–1112.

FARBER, S. M. & R. H. L. Wilson, Eds. 1966. The Challenge to Women: The Biological Avalanche. Basic Books, Inc. New York, N. Y.

FIRST INTERNATIONAL CONFERENCE ON FAMILY PLANNING PROGRAMS, PLANNING COMMITTEE. 1966. Family Planning Programs. University of Chicago Press. Chicago Ill.

FORD, C. S. 1952. Control of conception in cross-cultural perspective. Ann, N. Y. Acad. Sci. 54:763–768.

FREEDMAN, R., Ed. 1964. Population: The Vital Revolution. Doubleday. New York, N. Y.

FREEDMAN, R., P. K. WHELPTON & A. A. CAMPBELL. 1959. Family Planning, Sterility, and Population Growth. McGraw-Hill Book Co. New York, N. Y.

*FRYER, P. 1965. The Birth Controllers. Secker and Warburg. London, England.

*GEBHARD, P. H., W. B. POMEROY, C. MARTIN & C. CHRISTENSON. 1958. Pregnancy, Birth and Abortion. (Hoeber) Harper & Row. New York, N. Y.

*GILMORE, C. P. 1969. Something better than the pill? N. Y. Times Mag. July 20:6.

GLASS, D. V. & D. E. C. EVERSLEY, Eds. 1965. Population in History. Aldine Press, Chicago, Ill.

GOLDBERG, D. & C. H. COOMBS. Some applications of unfolding theory to fertility analysis. Emerging Techniques in Demographic Analysis. Milbank Memorial Fund Round Table.

GRABILL, W. H., C. V. KISER & P. K. WHELPTON. 1958. The Fertility of American Women. John Wiley & Sons, Inc. New York, N. Y.

*GRAHAM, H. 1951. Eternal Eve: The History of Gynecology and Obstetrics. Doubleday. New York, N. Y.

GREEP, R. O., Ed. 1963. Human Fertility and Population Problems. Schenkman. Cambridge, Mass.

*GUTTMACHER, A. F., Ed. 1967. The Case for Legalized Abortion Now. Diablo Press. Berkeley, Calif.

*HAMILTON, V. C. 1940. Some sociologic and psychologic observations on abortion. Amer. J. Obstet. Gynecol. 39(6):919–928.

*HAMILTON, V. C. 1941. Some observations on the contraceptive behavior of abortion patients. Human Fert. 5:37–41.

HARDIN, G., Ed. 1964. Population, Evolution & Birth Control. W. H. Freeman. San Francisco, Calif.

*HARDIN, G. 1966. The history and future of birth control. Perspect. Biol. Med. 10(1).

*HARDIN, G. 1967. Semantic aspects of abortion. ETC 24(3).

*HARDIN, G. 1968. Abortion – or compulsory pregnancy? J. Marr. Fam. 30(2).

HAUSER, P. M., Ed. 1963. The Population Dilemma. Prentice-Hall. Englewood Cliffs, N. J.

HAUSER, P. M. & O. D. DUNCAN, Eds. 1959. The Study of Population: An Inventory and Appraisal. University of Chicago Press. Chicago, Ill.

*HAVEMANN, E. K. 1967. Birth Control: A Special Time-Life Report. Time-Life. New York, N. Y.

*HIMES, N. A. 1963. A Medical History of Contraception. Gamut Press, New York, N. Y.

*INTERNATIONAL CONFERENCE ON ABORTION. 1968. The Terrible Choice: The Abortion Dilemma. Proceedings, Fall, 1967. Bantam Press. New York, N. Y.

*KARMEL, M. 1959. Thank You, Dr. Lamaze. J. B. Lippincott Co. Philadelphia, Pa.

KISER, C. V., Ed. 1962. Research in Family Planning. Princeton University Press. Princeton, N. J.

KISER, C. V., W. H. GRABILL & A. A. CAMPBELL. 1968. Trends and Variations in Fertility in the United States. Harvard University Press. Cambridge, Mass.

KOYA, Y. 1963. Pioneering in Family Planning. Japan Medical Publishers. Tokyo, Japan.

*LADER, L. 1966. Abortion. Bobbs-Merrill. New York, N. Y.

LANDER, L. 1955. The Margaret Sanger Story and the Fight for Birth Control. Doubleday. Garden City, N. Y.

*LaSAGNA, L. 1968. Life, Death and the Doctor. Alfred A. Knopf. New York, N. Y.

LEE, N. H. 1969. The Search for an Abortionist. University of Chicago Press, Chicago, Ill.

*LUCAS, R. 1968. Federal constitutional limitations on the enforcement and administration of state abortion statutes. N. C. Law Rev. 46(4).

MAIR, G. F., Ed. 1949. Studies in Population. Princeton University Press. Princeton, N. J.

McMAHAN, C. A. 1951. An empirical test of three hypotheses concerning the human sex ratio at birth in the United States, 1915—1948. Milbank Mem. Fund Quart. 29:273—293.

MEAD, M., *et al.* 1967. The Peaceful Revolution: Birth Control and the Changing Status of Women. Planned Parenthood-World Population. New York, N. Y.

*MEAD, M., *et al.* 1969. Voluntary population control? Three experts debate possibility. Planned Parenthood News 1(2):3.

MEIER, R. L. 1959. Modern Science and the Human Fertility Problem. John Wiley & Sons, Inc. New York, N. Y.

MILBANK MEMORIAL FUND. 1952. Approaches to Problems of High Fertility in Agrarian Societies. Milbank Memorial Fund, New York, N. Y.

MORAN, W. E., Ed. 1965. Population Growth — Threat to Peace? P. J. Kenedy & Sons. New York, N. Y.

*MOSKIN, J. R. 1969. The new contraceptive society. Look. Feb. 4:50—53.

MUDD, S., Ed. 1965. The Population Crisis: Implications and Plans for Action. Indiana University Press. Bloomington, Ind.

MYRDAL, A. 1968. Nation and Family: The Swedish Experiment in Democratic Family and Population Policy. Massachusetts Institute of Technology Press. Cambridge, Mass.

*NATIONAL OBSERVER. 1966. The Pill and Its Impact. National Observer Newsbook. New York, N. Y.

*NEUBARDT, S. 1967. A Concept of Contraception. Trident Press. New York, N. Y.

*NEWTON, N. 1955. Maternal Emotions. Harper & Row. New York, N. Y.

*OSOFSKY, H. The Pregnant Teenager. Charles C Thomas Publ. Springfield, Ill.

*PETERSEN, W. 1964. The Politics of Population. Doubleday. New York, N. Y.

PLANNED PARENTHOOD-WORLD POPULATION. A Selected Bibliography for Professionals on Family Planning and Related Subjects. Planned Parenthood, New York, N. Y.

POHLMAN, E. 1968. The timing of first births: A review of effects. Eugen. Quart. 15(4):252—263.

POHLMAN, E. W. 1967. Birth Timing and Spacing: Research and Recommendations. Mimeo.

POHLMAN, E. W. 1967. Unwanted conceptions: Research on undesirable consequences. Eugen. Quart. 14:143–154.

POLGAR, S. 1965. The impact of new contraceptive methods in impoverished neighborhoods of New York — Rationale and plan of research. Paper, Ann. Meet. Population Ass. Amer.

RAINWATER, L. 1967. Family planning in cross-national perspective: An overview. J. Soc. Issues 23:1–12.

RAINWATER, L. & K. WEINSTEIN. 1960. And the Poor Get Children: Sex Contraception and Family Planning in the Working Class. Quadrangle Books. Chicago, Ill.

*RAINWATER, L., *et al*. 1965. Family Design: Marital Sexuality, Family Size, and Contraception. Aldine Press. New York, N. Y.

ROCK, J. 1963. The Time Has Come. Alfred A. Knopf. New York, N. Y.

RODGERS, D. A., F. J. ZIEGLER, J. ALTROCCHI & N. LEVY. 1965. A longitudinal study of the psycho-social effects of vasectomy. J. Marr. Fam. 27:59–64.

ROSEN, H., Ed. 1954. Therapeutic Abortion. Julian Press. New York, N. Y.

*ROSSI, A. 1966. Abortion laws and their victims. Trans-action. Sept.-Oct.

*ROSSI, A. 1969. Abortion and social change. Dissent. July-Aug.: 338–346.

*SCHENK, R. U. 1968. Let's think about abortion. Cath. World: 207.

*SCHUR, E. M. 1955. Abortion and the social system. Soc. Prob. Oct.:94–99.

SHEPS, M. C. & J. C. RIDLEY. 1966. Public Health and Population Changes. Schenkman. Cambridge, Mass.

SHETTLES, L. B. 1961. Conception and birth sex ratios: A review. Obstet. Gynecol. 18:122–130.

SMITH, D. L. 1967. Abortion and the Law. Western Reserve Press. Cleveland, Ohio.

STEFFEN, T. & R. T. BUSHELL. 1964. The Contraceptive Industry and Its Environment. Carnegie Institute of Technology, Graduate School of Industrial Administration. Pittsburgh, Pa.

*STUART, M. & W. T. LIU. 1969. The Changing Woman: The Impact of Family Planning. Little, Brown & Co. Boston, Mass.

STYCOS, J. M. 1955. Family and Fertility in Puerto Rico. Columbia University Press. New York, N. Y.

STYCOS, J. M. 1963. Obstacles to programs of population control — Facts and fancies. Marr. Fam. Living 25:5–13.

STYCOS, J. M. 1964. The Cornell international population program. Milbank Mem. Fund Quart. 28.

STYCOS, J. M. & K. W. BACK. 1964. The Control of Human Fertility in Jamaica. Cornell University Press. Ithaca, N. Y.

*SWEDISH INSTITUTE FOR CULTURAL RELATIONS WITH FOREIGN COUNTRIES (Box 3306, Stockholm 3, Sweden). 1964. Therapeutic Abortion and the Law in Sweden.

*TANZER, D. 1968. Natural childbirth: Pain or peak experience? Psychol. Today. 2(5).

THIESSEN, D. D. & D. A. RODGERS. 1961. Population density and endocrine function. Psychol. Bull. 58:441–451.

THOMPSON, W. S. & D. T. LEWIS. 1965. Population Problems. 5th edit. McGraw-Hill Book Co. New York, N. Y.

TIETZE, C. 1960. Selected Bibliography of Contraception: 1940–1960. National Committee on Maternal Health. New York, N. Y.

TIETZE, C. 1962. Surgical Sterilization of Men and Women: A Selected Bibliography. National Committee on Maternal Health. New York, N. Y.

TIETZE, C. 1965. Bibliography of Fertility Control: 1950–1965. National Committee on Maternal Health. New York, N. Y.

TIETZE, C. 1965. History of contraceptive methods. J. Sex. Res. 1:69–85.

TIETZE, C. & H. LEHFELDT. 1961. Legal abortion in Eastern Europe. J. Amer. Med. Ass. 175:1149–1154.

*VINCENT, C. 1961. Unmarried Mothers. The Free Press. New York, N. Y.

WALDROP, M. F. & R. Q. BELL. 1966. Effects of family size and density on newborn characteristics. Amer. J. Orthopsychiat. 36(3): 544–550.

WEILER, H. 1959. Sex ratio and birth control. Amer. J. Sociol. 65:298–299.

WESTOFF, C. F., R. G. POTTER & P. C. SAGI. 1963. The Third Child. Princeton University Press. Princeton, N. J.

WHELPTON, P. K., A. A. CAMPBELL & J. PATTERSON. 1966. Fertility and Family Planning in the United States. Princeton University Press. Princeton, N. J.

*WHITE, R. B. 1966. Induced abortions: A survey of their psychiatric implications, complications, and indications. Tex. Rep. Biol. Med. 24(4):531–558.

WINSTON, S. 1932. Birth control and the sex ratio at birth. Amer. J. Sociol. 38:225–231.

*WOODSIDE, M. 1962. Attitudes of women abortionists. Howard J. 11(2).

Women in Society: Status and Legal Issues

*ANÉR, K. 1966. Swedish Women Today: A Personal Appraisal. Swedish Institute (Box 3306, Stockholm 3, Sweden).

ASTIN, H. S. 1969. The Woman Doctorate in America. Russell Sage. New York, N. Y.

BEBEL, A. 1910. Women and Socialism. Socialist Literature Co. New York, N. Y.

*BEECHER, C. E. 1842. A Treatise on Domestic Economy.

*BERGER, B. 1960. Working-Class Suburb. University of California Press. Berkeley, Calif.

*BERNARD, J. 1964. Academic Women. Pennsylvania State University Press. Philadelphia, Pa.

*BERREMAN, G. 1966. On the role of women. Bull. At. Sci., Nov.

BERRY, J. 1955. Life plans of college women. J. Nat. Ass. Deans Wom. 18:76—80.

BERRY, J. & S. EPSTEIN. 1963. Continuing Education of Women: Needs, Aspirations and Plans. The University of Missouri at Kansas City Press. Kansas City, Mo.

BROWN, D. R., Ed. 1968. Women in the Soviet Union. Teachers College. New York, N. Y.

BIRD, C. 1966. Let's draft women, too. Sat. Evening Post. June 18.

*BIRD, C. 1968. Born Female. David McKay Co. New York, N. Y.

*BOORSTIN, D. The Image.

BORCHERS, G. L. 1963. Some investigations concerning the status of faculty women in America. In: Women in College and University Teaching.

*BORGESE, E. M. 1962. The Ascent of Women. George Braziller, Inc. New York, N. Y.

BRECKENRIDGE, S. P. 1933. Women in the Twentieth Century — A Study of Their Political, Social and Economic Activities. McGraw-Hill Book Co. New York, N. Y.

*CASSARA, B. B., Ed. 1962. American Women: The Changing Image. Beacon Press. New York, N. Y.

CAVAN, S. 1956—1957. The status of women in the professions relative to the status of men. Quart. Amer. Interprofessional Inst. Winter.

COMMITTEE ON EDUCATION AND LABOR. 1948. Equal pay for equal work for women. Report of the United States House of Representatives, Subcommittee No. 4, of the Committee on Education and Labor. 80th Congress, 2nd Session. Feb. 9, 10, 11 & 13.

THE CONGRESSIONAL RECORD. 1966. Women are being deprived of legal rights by the Equal Employment Opportunity Commission. June 20.

DAEDALUS. 1964. The woman in America. Spring.

*DAHLSTROM, E., Ed. 1967. The Changing Roles of Men and Women. Duckworth. London, England.

DAVID, O. 1957. The Education of Women — Signs for the Future. American Council on Education. Washington, D. C.

De BEAUVOIR, S. 1953. The Second Sex. Translated by H. M. Parshley. Alfred A. Knopf. New York, N. Y.

DEGLER, C. N. 1964. Revolution without ideology: The changing place of women in America. Daedalus: 653—670.

*De RHAM, E. 1965. The Love Fraud. Clarkson Potter. New York, N. Y.

*DINGWALL, E. J. 1956. The American Woman.

*DITZION, S. 1953. Marriage, Morals and Sex in America — A History of Ideas. New York, N. Y.

DODGE, N. T. 1966. Women in the Soviet Economy. The John Hopkins Press. Baltimore, Md.

DOLAN, E. F. 1963. Higher education for women: Time for reappraisal. Higher Educ. Sept.

EQUAL EMPLOYMENT OPPORTUNITY COMMISSION. First Annual Digest of Legal Interpretations. July, 1965—July, 1967.

ELLMAN, M. 1968. Thinking About Women. Harcourt, Brace & World. New York, N. Y.

EPSTEIN, C. F. 1970. Woman's Place. Options and Limitations in Professional Careers. University of California Press. Berkeley, Calif.

*FANON, F. Studies in a Dying Colonialism.

*FANON, F. The Wretched of the Earth.

FARBER, S. & R. H. L. WILSON, Eds. 1963. The Potential of Women. McGraw-Hill Book Co. New York, N. Y.

*FENBERG, M. 1948. Blame Coke and Blackstone. Wom. Lawyers J. 34(2):7.

FIRKEL, E. 1963. Woman in the Modern World. Fides Publ. Notre Dame, Ind.

*FRANCIS, P. 1963. Legal Status of Women.

FRIEDAN, B. 1960. Women are people too! Good Housekeeping. Sept.

FRIEDAN, B. 1961. If one generation can ever tell another. Smith Alumnae Quart. Northampton, Mass. Winter.

*FRIEDAN, B. 1963. The Feminine Mystique. W. W. Norton. New York, N. Y.

*FROST, D. & A. JAY. 1969. Women. In: The English. Avon Books. New York, N. Y.

GALLEN, R. T. 1965. Wives' Legal Rights. Dell Publ. Co. New York, N. Y.

GINZBERG, E. 1966. Life Styles of Educated Women. Columbia University Press. New York, N. Y.

GINZBERG, E. & A. M. YOHALEM. 1966. Educated American Women: Self-Portraits. Columbia University Press. New York, N. Y.

HALLE, F. 1933. Women in Soviet Russia. Routledge. London, England.

*HERSCHBERGER, R. 1948. Adam's Rib. Pellegrini and Cudahy. New York, N. Y.

JONES, B. & J. BROWN. 1968. Toward a Female Liberation Movement. New England Free Press. Cambridge, Mass.

*KALVESTEN, A. 1966. Social Structure of Sweden. Swedish Institute (Box 3306, Stockholm 3, Sweden).

*KANOWITZ, L. 1967. Law and the married woman. St. Louis U. Law J. 12:3.

KANOWITZ, L. 1967. Sex-based discrimination in American law and the single girl. St. Louis U. Law J. 11:293—330.

*KANOWITZ, L. 1969. Women and the Law, The Unfinished Revolution. University of New Mexico Press. Albuquerque, N. M.

KIRKPATRICK, C. 1938. Nazi Germany. Its Women and Family Life. Bobbs-Merrill. Indianapolis, Ind.

KOMAROVSKY, M. 1953. Women in the Modern World: Their Education and Their Dilemmas. Little, Brown & Co. Boston, Mass.

*KOMAROVSKY, M. 1964. Blue-Collar Marriage. Random House. New York, N. Y.

LAMSON, P. L. 1968. Few are Chosen. American Women in Political Life Today. Houghton-Mifflin Co. Boston, Mass.

*LEIJON, A. Swedish Women — Swedish Men. Swedish Institute for Cultural Relations with Foreign Countries (Box 3306, Stockholm 3, Sweden).

LEONARD, M. C., Ed. 1963. Equal Rights Amendment: Questions and Answers Prepared by the Research Department of the National Women's Party. Document No. 164. Government Printing Office.

*LESSING, D. 1960. In Pursuit of the English.

LEWIS, E. E. 1968. Developing Woman's Potential. Iowa State University Press. Ames, Iowa.

*LEWIS, O. 1961. The Children of Sanchez. Vintage Books. New York, N. Y.

*LEWIS, O. 1965. LaVida. Vintage Books. New York, N. Y.

LIFTON, R. J., Ed. 1964. The Woman in America. Beacon Press. Boston, Mass.

*LINNER, B. Sex and Society in Sweden. Pantheon Books. New York, N. Y.

LUCE, C. B. 1967. Is it now or never for women? McCall's. April.

*McVEETY, J. 1967. Law and the single woman. Wom. Lawyers. J. 53(1):10.

*MICHAEL, D. 1965. Cybernation. Center for the Study of Democratic Institutions. Santa Barbara, Calif.

MILLETT, K. 1970. Sexual Politics. Doubleday. New York, N. Y.

MINNEAPOLIS TRIBUNE. 1967. Women claim job laws "protect" them too much. Jan. 15.

MONK, D. 1970. Defining the new feminists. Los Angeles Times. Jan. 4.

*MORRIS, R. B. 1958. Studies in the History of American Law: 126–201.

*MURRAY, P. & M. EASTWOOD. 1965. Jane Crow and the law: Sex discrimination and Title VII. George Washington Law Rev. 34(2): 232.

*NEWCOMER, M. 1959. A Century of Higher Education for American Women. New York, N. Y.

NEW YORK TIMES MAGAZINE. 1960. The woman with brains. Jan. 17.

*PATAI, R., Ed. 1967. Women in the Modern World. The Free Press. New York, N. Y.

*PILPEL, H. & T. ZAVIN. 1962. Your Marriage and the Law. P. F. Collier, Inc. New York, N. Y.

POLLACK, J. H. 1965. Girl dropouts: a neglected national tragedy. Parade. Sept. 26.

*POLLAK, O. 1950. The Criminality of Women. University of Pennsylvania Press. Philadelphia, Pa.

*POLSTER, E. 1967. Conscription: The war on women and children. (Speech available from Women's International League for Peace and Freedom, 2006 Walnut St., Philadelphia, Pa. 19103.)

*POTTER, D. 1962. American Women and American Character. Stetson University Press. De Land, Fla.

*PRUETTE, L. 1924. Woman and Leisure. A Study of Waste. E. P. Dutton & Co. New York, N. Y.

*RAINWATER, L., R. P. COLEMAN & G. HANDEL. 1959. Workingman's Wife: Her Personality, World, and Life Style. Oceana Publ. New York, N. Y.

*REICH, W. 1945. The Sexual Revolution. Farrar, Straus & Giroux. New York, N. Y.

*RIEGEL, R. E. 1968. American Feminists. University of Kansas Press. Lawrence, Kan.

RIESMAN, D. 1965. Some dilemmas of women's education. Educ. Rec. Fall.

*ROSSEL, J. 1965. Women in Sweden. Swedish Institute (Box 3306, Stockholm 3, Sweden).

ROSSI, A. S. 1964. Equality between the sexes: An immodest proposal. Daedalus. Spring:607–652.

ROSSI, A. S. 1969. Sex equality: The beginnings of ideology. The Humanist. Sept./Oct.

SCOFIELD, N. E. 1960. Some changing roles of women in suburbia: A social anthropological case study. Trans. N. Y. Acad. Sci. 22(6).

*SCOTT, A. F. 1962. The "new women" in the new South. S. Atlantic Quart. 61.

*SIMON, R. J., S. M. CLARK & K. GALWAY. 1967. The woman Ph.D.: A recent profile. Soc. Prob. 15(2).

*SIMON, R. J., S. CLARK & L. L. TIFFT. 1966. Of nepotism, marriage, and the pursuit of an academic career. Sociol. Educa. 39(4).

*SNOW, H. 1968. Women in Modern China. Humanities Press. New York, N. Y.

*SPIRO, M. Kibbutz.

STERN, E. M. 1949. Women are household slaves. Amer. Mercury. Jan.

STRACHEY, R., Ed. 1936. Our Freedom and its Results. Hogarth Press. London, England.

*SWEDISH INSTITUTE FOR CULTURAL RELATIONS WITH FOREIGN COUNTRIES. 1965. Swedish Divorce Laws. (Box 3306, Stockholm 3, Sweden).

*SWEDISH INSTITUTE FOR CULTURAL RELATIONS WITH FOREIGN COUNTRIES. 1968. The Status of Women in Sweden: Report to the United Nations. (Box 3306, Stockholm 3, Sweden.)

*TARBELL, I. 1912. The business of Being a Woman. MacMillan Co. New York, N. Y.

THIS WEEK. 1967. Sex and civil rights. March 19.

UNITED NATIONS. 1963. Political rights of women in member nations of the United Nations. In: Women in the World Today. Int. Rep. 2, United Nations Rept. A/5456. Reprinted by Women's Bureau. Washington, D. C.

UNITED STATES DEPARTMENT OF LABOR, BUREAU OF EMPLOYMENT SECURITY. 1942. Occupations suitable for women. Washington, D. C.

*UNITED STATES DEPARTMENT OF LABOR, WOMEN'S BUREAU. Know Your Rights. Washington, D. C.

*UNITED STATES DEPARTMENT OF LABOR, WOMEN'S BUREAU. Leaflet No. 10. Washington, D. C.

WALL STREET JOURNAL. 1967. Women's groups fight last vestiges of bias on job, before the law. May 23.

WARE, C. 1970. Woman Power: The Movement for Women's Liberation. Tower Publications, Inc. New York, N. Y.

*WEST, A. 1968. Who takes advantage of American women? Men. Vogue. May:198.

*WHITE, L. 1950. Educating Our Daughters. Harpers. New York, N. Y.

WOERISHOFFER, C. 1945. Women during the war and after. Graduate Department of Social Economy and Social Research. Bryn Mawr College. Bryn Mawr, Pa.

*WOLFF, J. 1958. What Makes Women Buy. McGraw-Hill Book Co. New York, N. Y.

WOMEN'S BUREAU. 1966. College Women Seven Years After Graduation. Bulletin 292. Washington, D. C.

Women and the World of Work

ABBOTT, E. 1910. Women in Industry: A Study in American Economic History.

ASTIN, H. S. 1969. The Woman Doctorate in America. Russell Sage. New York, N. Y.

*BAGDIKIAN, B. H. 1966. Who is sabotaging day care for our children? Ladies Home J. Nov.:86.

*BAKER, E. F. 1964. Technology and Women's Work. Columbia University Press. New York, N. Y.

*BAKER, M. 1962. Women who work. Int. Soc. Rev. Summer.

*BEECHER, C. E. 1842. A Treatise on Domestic Economy.

*BENJAMIN, L. 1966. So You Want to be a Working Mother! McGraw-Hill Book Co. New York, N. Y.

BERRY, J. 1955. Life plans of college women. J. Nat. Ass. Deans Wom. 18:76–80.

BIRD, C. 1967. What we are finding out about working mothers. Woman's Day. Sept.

*BIRD, C. 1968. Born Female. David McKay Co. New York, N. Y.

*BLOOD, R. O. Long-range causes and consequences of the employment of married women. J. Marr. Fam. 27(1).

BLOUSTEIN, E. J. 1968. Man's work goes from sun to sun but woman's work is never done. Psychol. Today 1(10):38.

*BOONE, G. 1942. The Woman's Trade Union League.

BORCHERS, G. L. 1963. Some investigations concerning the state of faculty women in America. In: Women in College and University Teaching.

BORING, E. G. 1951. The woman problem. Amer. Psychol. 6:679.

BOYNTON, P. L. & R. D. WOOLWINE. 1942. The relationship between the economic status of high school girls and their vocational wishes and expectations. J. Appl. Psychol. 26:399—415.

*BROWNLEE, J. 1967. Where is the professional woman? Wom. Lawyers J. 53(1):14.

BRYAN, A. I. & E. G. BORING. 1947. Women in American psychology: Factors affecting their professional careers. Amer. Psychol. 2:3—20.

CAIN, G. G. 1966. Married Women in the Labor Force: An Economic Analysis. Unviersity of Chicago Press. Chicago, Ill.

CAVAN, S. 1956—1957. The status of women in the professions relative to the status of men. Quart. Amer. Interprofessional Inst. Winter.

COCKBURN, P. 1967. Women university graduates in continuing education and employment. An exploratory study initiated by the Canadian Federation of University Women, 1966. Toronto, Canada.

COLLINS, J. 1969. Women in the universities. The Radical Teacher. Dec. 30:13—14.

COMMITTEE ON EDUCATION AND LABOR. 1948. Equal pay for equal work for women. Report of the United States House of Representatives, Subcommittee No. 4, of the Committee on Education and Labor. 80th Congress, 2nd Session. Feb. 9, 10, 11 & 13.

THE CONGRESSIONAL RECORD. 1966. Women are being deprived of legal rights by the Equal Employment Opportunity Commission. June 20.

COOPER, J. D. 1964. A Woman's Guide to Part-Time Jobs. Dolphin Books. New York, N. Y.

COTTON, D. W. 1965. The Case for the Working Mothers. Stein & Day. New York, N. Y.

*CUSSLER, M. 1958. The Woman Executive. Harcourt, Brace & World. New York, N. Y.

*DEXTER, E. A. 1950. Career Woman of America, 1776—1840. Marshall Jones Co. Francetown, N. H.

*DICHTER, E. The Strategy of Desire.

DUN'S REVIEW. 1966. Women — Industry's newest challenge. August.

EQUAL EMPLOYMENT OPPORTUNITY COMMISSION. 1966. The First Annual Report. House Document No. 86.

EPSTEIN, C. F. 1970. Woman's Place: Options and Limits in Professional Careers. University of California Press. Berkeley, Calif.

*FAVA, S. 1960 The status of women in professional sociology. Amer. Sociol. Rev. 25:271—276.

FEDERAL WOMAN'S AWARD STUDY GROUP ON CAREER FOR WOMEN PROGRESS REPORT TO THE PRESIDENT. 1967. March 3.

FLEXNER, E. Woman's Work in America.

HARBESON, G. E. 1967. Choice and Challenge for the American Woman. Schenkman. Cambridge, Mass.

*HARTMAN, S. 1969. Should wives work? McCall's. Feb.:57.

*HATTERER, L. J. 1966. The woman artist. In: The Artist in Society: Problems and Treatment of the Creative Personality. Grove Press. New York, N. Y.

*HENRY, A. 1923. Women and the Labor Movement.

HEYWOOD, A. 1951. There is a Right Job for Every Woman. Doubleday & Co. Garden City, N. Y.

INDUSTRIAL RELATIONS. 1968. Women in the labor force. 7(3).

JEPHCOTT, P., N. SEEAR & J. H. SMITH. 1962. Married Women Working. Allen & Unwin. London, England.

KENISTON, E. & K. KENISTON. 1964. An American anachronism: The image of women and work. Amer. Scholar.33:355–375.

KINGSBURY, S. H. & M. FAIRCHILD. 1935. Factory, Family and Women in the Soviet Union. G. P. Putnam. New York, N. Y.

KUNDSIN, R. B. 1965. Where are our women in science? Howard Med. Alumni Bull. Winter.

KYRK, H. 1946. Who works and why. Ann. Amer. Acad. Pol. Soc. Sci. May.

LAMBECK, R. 1968. 380 Part-Time Jobs for Women. Bell Publishing Co. New York, N. Y.

*MARMOR, J. 1968. Women in medicine: importance of the formative years. J. Amer. Med. Wom. Ass.23(7).

*MATTFELD, J. A. & C. G. VAN AKEN, Eds. 1965. Women and the Scientific Professions. Massachusetts Institute of Technology Press. Cambridge, Mass.

MILLER, M. M. 1961. Women in university teaching. J. Amer. Ass. Univ. Women 54.

MINCER, J. 1962. Labor force participation of married women. In: Aspects of Labor Economics. Princeton University Press. Princeton, N. J.

MINNEAPOLIS TRIBUNE. 1967. Women claim job laws "protect" them too much. Jan. 15.

*MORSE, N. S. & R. S. WEISS. 1955. The function and meaning of work and the job. Amer. Sociol. Rev. 20:191–198.

*MURRAY, P. & M. EASTWOOD. 1965. Jane Crow and the law: Sex discrimination and Title VII. George Washington Law Rev. 34(2): 232.

MYRDAL, A. & K. VIOLA. 1956. Women's Two Roles: Home and Work. Routledge and Kegan Paul. London, England.

*NATIONAL MANPOWER COUNCIL. 1957. Womanpower and Work in the Lives of Married Women.

NATIONAL SCIENCE FOUNDATION. 1961. Women in Scientific Careers. Govt. Printing Office. Washington, D. C.

NEFF, W. F. 1929. Victorian Working Women. Columbia University Press. New York, N. Y.

NEW YORK POST.1967. New jobs for women: a survey. Aug. 21.

NEW YORK TIMES. 1965. De-sexing the job market (Editorial). Aug. 21.

*NYE, F. I. & L. W. HOFFMAN, Eds. 1963. The Employed Mother in America. Rand-McNally. New York, N. Y.

O'NEILL, B. P. 1965. Careers for Women after Marriage and Children. MacMillan Co. New York, N. Y.

ORDEN, S. & N. BRADBURN. 1969. Working wives and marriage happiness. Amer. J. Sociol. Jan.

PARRISH, J. 1962. Women in top level teaching and research. J. Amer. Ass. U. Women 55:102.

PETERSON, E. T. 1958. The impact of maternal employment on the mother-daughter relationship and on the daughter's role orientation. Unpublished doctoral dissertation. The University of Michigan. Ann Arbor, Mich.

PETERSON, E. T. 1964. Working women. Daedalus 93:671–699.

*PINCH-BECK, I. Women Workers in the Industrial Revolution.

*PRESSMAN, S. 1968. Sex discrimination in employment and what you can do about it. Wom. Lawyers J. 54(4):6.

ROSENFELD, C. & V. C. PERRELLA. 1965. Why women start and stop working: A study in mobility. Monthly Labor Rev. Sept.

ROSSI, A. 1967. Working wives: How well is business talking their language? Management Rev. April.

ROYSTER, V. 1964. The work mystique. Wall St. J. June 24.

*RUDERMAN, F. Child Care and Working Mothers. Child Welfare League of America. New York, N. Y.

RUSSO, Jr., S. A. & W. LAAS. 1968. Women! Business Needs You! A Back-to-Business Guide for Modern Women. Popular Library. New York, N. Y.

*SCHREINER, O. 1911. Woman and Labour. Fisher Unwin. London, England.

SCOBEY, J. & L. P. McGRATH. 1968. Creative Careers for Women. A Handbook of Sources and Ideas for Part-Time Jobs. Essandess Special Editons (Simon & Schuster). New York, N. Y.

SCOFIELD, N. E. & B. KLARMAN. 1968. So You Want to Go Back to Work! Random House. New York, N. Y.

*SIMON, R. J., S. M. CLARK & K. GALWAY. 1967. The woman Ph.D.: A recent profile. Soc. Probl. 15(2).

*SIMON, R. J., S. CLARK & L. L. TIFFT. 1966. Of nepotism, marriage and the pursuit of an academic career. Sociol. Educ. 39(4).

SLOCUM, W. L. & L. T. EMPEY. 1957. Occupational planning by high school and college girls. J. Home Econ. 49:125–126.

*SMITH, G. 1964. Help Wanted: Female, A study of Demand and Supply in a Local Job Market for Women. Rutgers Institute of Management and Labor Relations. New Brunswick, N. J.

*SMUTS, R. W. 1959. Women and Work in America. Columbia University Press. New York, N. Y.

SOCIAL RESEARCH, INC. Bringing women back to work: A study of the woman at home and the manpower white glove girl. Social Research, Inc. Chicago, Ill.

SOUTHARD, H. F. 1960. Mothers' dilemma: To work or not? N. Y. Times Mag. July 17.

*SPRUILL, J. C. Women's Life and Work in the Southern Colonies. University of North Carolina Press. Chapel Hill, N. C.

STERN, M. B. 1963. We the Women: Career Firsts of Nineteenth Century America. Schulte Publishing Co. New York, N. Y.

STOLLENWERK, T. 1968. Back to Work, Ladies: A Career Guide for the Mature Woman. Pilot Books. New York, N. Y.

STOLZ, L. M. 1960. Effects of maternal employment on children: Evidence from research. Child Develop. 31(4):749–782.

SYSIHARJU, A. 1960. Equality, Home and Work: A Socio-psychological Study on Finnish Student Women's Attitudes Toward the Woman's Role in Society. Mikkelissa. Helsinki, Finland.

TANGRI, S. S. 1969. Role-innovation in occupational choice. Doctoral dissertation. University of Michigan. Ann Arbor, Mich.

UNITED STATES DEPARTMENT OF LABOR, BUREAU OF EMPLOYMENT SECURITY. 1942. Occupations suitable for women. Washington, D. C.

UNITED STATES DEPARTMENT OF LABOR. 1969. Handbook on Women Workers. Bulletin 294. Women's Bureau. Washington, D. C.

UNITED STATES DEPARTMENT OF LABOR, WAGE AND LABOR STANDARDS ADMINISTRATION, WOMEN'S BUREAU. 1968. Working Mothers and the Need for Child Care Services. June. Washington, D. C.

*UNITED STATES DEPARTMENT OF LABOR, WOMEN'S BUREAU. 1968. The Fuller Utilization of the Woman Physician. Washington, D. C.

*UNITED STATES DEPARTMENT OF LABOR, WOMEN'S BUREAU. Know Your Rights. Washington, D. C.

*UNITED STATES DEPARTMENT OF LABOR, WOMEN'S BUREAU. Leaflet no. 10. Washington, D. C.

U. S. NEWS & WORLD REPORT. 1967. Where job changes will be best in the years just ahead. Jan. 2.

WALL STREET JOURNAL. 1967. Women's groups fight last vestiges of bias on job, before the law. May 23.

*WEIL, M. W. 1961. An analysis of the factors influencing married women's actual or planned work participation. Amer. Sociol. Rev. 26:91–96.

*WHITE, J. J. 1967. Women in the law. Mich. Law Rev. 65:1051.

WINTER, E. L. 1967. Women at Work: Every Woman's Guide to Successful Employment. Simon & Schuster. New York, N. Y.

WOERISHOFFER, C. 1945. Women during the war and after. Graduate Department of Social Economy and Social Research, Bryn Mawr College. Bryn Mawr, Pa.

*WOLFLE, D. 1954. America's Resources of Specialized Talent.

*WOMEN IN THE (SERVICE) INDUSTRY: A MINORITY RE-PORT. 1969. Inst. Mag. 64(3):87–110.

WOMEN'S BUREAU. 1966. College Women Seven Years after Graduation. Bulletin 292.

ZISSUS, C. 1964. A study of the life planning of 550 freshman women at Purdue Universtiy. J. Nat. Ass. Wom. Deans Couns. 27(4): 143–159.

Psychological Issues and Problems

ABRAHAM, K. 1922. Manifestations of ₋he female castration complex. Int. J. Psychoanal. 3.

AGRIST, S. S. 1969. The study of sex roles. J. Soc. Issues 25:215.

BAILYN, L. 1964. Notes on the role of choice in the psychology of professional women. Daedalus. Spring: 700–710.

*BALINT, A. 1937. Psychology of menstruation. Psychoanal. Quart. May.

BARUCH, R. 1967. The achievement motive in women: Implications for career development. J. Personality Soc. Psychol. 5(3): 260–267.

*BENEDEK, T. 1952. Psychosexual Function in Women. Ronald Press. New York, N. Y.

*BERNARD, J. 1968. The Sex Game. Prentice-Hall. Englewood Cliffs, N. J.

BIBRING, G. L. 1959. Some considerations of the psychological processes in pregnancy. Psychoanal. Stud. Child. 14:113–121.

BIBRING, G. L., T. F. DWYER, D. S. HUNTINGTON & A. F. VALENSTINE. 1961. A study of the psychosocial processes in pregnancy and of the earliest mother-child relationship. Psychoanal. Stud. Child. 16:9–72.

*BONAPARTE, M. 1965. Female Sexuality. Grove Press. New York, N. Y.

BOYNTON, P. L. & R. D. WOOLWINE. 1942. The relationship between the economic status of high school girls and their vocational wishes and expectations. J. Appl. Psychol. 26:399–415.

*BRENTON, M. 1967. The American Male: A Penetrating Look at the Masculinity Crisis. Coward-McCann. New York, N. Y.

BROWN, N. O. 1959. Life Against Death. Random House. New York, N. Y.

*CHADWICK, M. 1932. The Psychological Effects of Menstruation. Nervous and Mental Disease Publ. Co. New York, N. Y.

CHAPMAN, J. D. 1968. The Feminine Mind and Body. Citadel Press. New York, N. Y.

COHN, D. L. 1943. Love in America, An Informal Study of Manners and Morals in American Marriage. Simon & Schuster. New York, N. Y.

*De MARTINO, M. F., Ed. 1966. Sexual Behavior and Personality Characertistics. Grove Press. New York, N. Y.

DePREE, S. 1962. The influence of parental achievement expectations and role definitions on achievement motive development in girls. Unpublished honors thesis. University of Michigan. Ann Arbor, Mich.

*DEUTSCHE, H. 1945. The Psychology of Women, A Psychoanalytic Interpretation. (2 vol.) Grune & Stratton. New York, N. Y.

*DEXTER, L. A. 1964. The Tyranny of Schooling. Basic Books. New York, N. Y.

DHULEY, N. B. 1965. Masculine complex in adolescent girls. Psychol. Stud. 10(1):51−53.

ELLIS, A. 1955. The Folklore of Sex. New York, N. Y.

*ELLIS, A. 1962. The American Sexual Tragedy.

*ELLIS, H. Man and Woman.

ERIKSON, E. 1950. Childhood and Society. W. W. Norton. New York, N. Y.

ERIKSON, E. 1959. Identity and the life cycle, selected papers. Psychol. Issues 1(1).

ERIKSON, E. 1964. Insight and Responsibility. W. W. Norton. New York, N. Y.

ERIKSON, E. 1968. Identity Youth and Crisis. W. W. Norton, New York, N. Y.

ERIKSON, E. H. 1964. Inner and outer space: Reflections on womanhood. Daedalus. Spring:582−606.

*FLUGEL, J. C. 1934. Men and Their Motives. London, England.

FORD, C. S. & F. A. BEACH. 1951. Patterns of Sexual Behavior. Harper Bros. New York, N. Y.

FRENCH, E. G. & G. S. LESSER. 1964. Some characteristics of achievement motives in women. J. Abnorm. Soc. Psychol. 68:119−128.

FREUD, S. 1962. Three Contributions to the Theory of Sex. Translated by J. Strachey. W. W. Norton. New York, N. Y.

FREUD, S. 1965. Feminity, lecture. XXXIII. In: New Introductory Lectures on Psychoanalysis. W. W. Norton. New York, N. Y.

FROMM, E. Sex and character: The Kinsey report viewed from the standpoint of psychoanalysis. In: Sexual Behavior in American Society.

*GAGNON, J. H. 1965. Sexuality and sexual learning in the child. Psychiatry 8:212−228.

GHEI, S. N. 1966. Needs of Indian and American college females. J. Soc. Psychol. 69:3−12.

*GOLDBERG, P. 1968. Are women prejudiced against women? Trans-action. April.

GOODE, W. J. 1960. Norm commitment and conformity to role-status obligations. Amer. J. Sociol. 66:246−248.

*GORDON, R. E. & K. K. GORDON. 1960. The Split Level Trap.

*GRAY, M. 1967. The Normal Woman. Scribner's. New York, N. Y.

*HALL, M. H. 1969. A conversation with Masters and Johnson. Psychol. Today 3(2):50−58.

*HART, H. & E. HART. 1935. Personalities and the Family. New York, N. Y.

HARTLEY, R. E. 1960. Children's concepts of male and female roles. Merrill-Palmer Quart. 6:83−91.

HARTLEY, R. E. 1964. A development view of female sex-role definition and identification. Merrill-Palmer Quart. 10:3–16.

HEIST, P. 1962. The motivation of college women today: A closer look. J. Amer. Ass. Univ. Women 55.

HELSON, R. M. 1961. Creativity, sex, and mathematics. Proc. Conf. Creative Person, Oct. 13-17. Institute for Personality Assessment and Research and University Extension. University of California, Liberal Arts Department. Berkeley, Calif.

*HILLIARD, M. 1960. Women and Fatigue. Doubleday & Co. New York, N. Y.

*HIMELHOCK, J. & S. F. FAVA, Eds. 1955. Sexual Behavior in American Society. W. W. Norton. New York, N. Y.

HORNER, M. 1969. Fail: Bright women. Psychol. Today. Nov.

HORNER, M. S. 1968. Sex differences in achievement motive and performance in competitive and non-competitive situations. Unpublished doctoral dissertation. The University of Michigan. Ann Arbor, Mich.

*HORNEY, K. Female Psychology. W. W. Norton. New York, N. Y.

*HORNEY, K. Feminine psychology. In: New Ways in Psychoanalysis. W. W. Norton. New York, N. Y.

JAHODA, M. & J. HAVEL. 1955. Psychological problems of women in different social roles – A case history of problem formulation in research. Educ. Rec. 36:325–333.

KAGIN, J. 1964. The acquisition and significance of sex-typing. In: Rev. Child Develop. Res. M. Hoffman, Ed. Russell Sage. New York, N. Y.

KALISH, R. A., M. MALONEY & A. ARKOFF. 1966. Cross-cultural comparisons of college student marital-role preferences. J. Soc. Psychol. 68:41–47.

KESTENBERG, J. 1956. On the development of maternal feelings in early childhood. Psychoanal. Stud. Child. 11.

KESTENBERG, J. 1956. Vicissitudes of female sexuality. J. Amer. Psychoanal. Ass. 4:453–476.

*KINSEY, A. C. 1953. Sexual Behavior in the Human Female. W. B. Saunders Co. Philadelphia, Pa.

*KLEIN, V. 1946. The Feminine Character, History of an Ideology. Kegan Paul. London, England.

KOMAROVSKY, M. 1946. Cultural contradictions and sex roles. Amer. J. Sociol. 52:184–189.

KOMAROVSKY, M. 1950. Functional analysis of sex roles. Sociol. Rev. August.

*KRONHAUSEN, D. & E. KRONHAUSEN. The Sexually Responsive Female.

KRICH, A., Ed. 1965. The Sexual Revolution, Pioneer Writings on Sex. (2 vol.) Dell Publ. Co. New York, N. Y.

*KURTZ, R. M. 1968. Body image – Male and female. Trans-action. Dec.:25–27.

*LAING, R. D. 1960. The Divided Self: An Existential Study in Sanity and Madness. Tavistock-Barnes and Noble. New York, N. Y.

*LEGMAN, G. 1968. The Rationale of the Dirty Joke: An Analysis of Sexual Humor. Grove Press. New York, N. Y.

LIPINSKY, B. G. 1965. Sex-role conflict and achievement motivation in college women. Dissertation. University of Cincinnati. Cincinnati, Ohio.

LUNDBERG, F. & M. FARNHAM. 1947. Modern Women: The Lost Sex, Grossett & Dunlap. New York, N. Y.

*MACCOBY, E., Ed. 1966. The Development of Sex Differences. Stanford, Calif.

MALINOWSKI, B. 1927. Sex and Repression in Savage Society. The Humanities Press. New York, N. Y.

MASLOW, A. H. 1939. Dominance, personality and social behavior in women. J. Soc. Psychol. 10:3–39.

*MASLOW, A. H. 1942. Self-esteem (dominance feeling) and sexuality in women. J. Soc. Psychol. 16:259–294.

*MASLOW, A. H. 1954. Motivation and Personality. Harper & Row. New York, N. Y.

*MASLOW, A. H. 1956. Self-actualizing people: A study of psychological health. In: Self: Exploration in Personal Growth. C. E. Moustakas, Ed. Harper & Row. New York, N. Y.

*MASTERS, W. H. & V. E. JOHNSON. 1966. Human Sexual Response. Little, Brown & Co. Boston, Mass.

MATHEWS, E. & D. V. TIEDEMAN. 1964. Attitudes toward career and marriage and the development of life style in young women. J. Counsel. Psychol. 11(4):375–384.

McKEE, J. P. & A. C. SHERRIFFS. 1959. Men's and women's belief, ideals and self-concepts. Amer. J. Sociol. 64:356–363.

MEAD, M. 1947. Age patterning in personality development. Amer. J. Orthopsychiatry 17(2): 231–240.

MEAD, M. 1949. Male and Female. William Morrow & Co. New York, N. Y.

MEAD, M. 1951. Cultural contexts of aging. In: No Time To Grow Old. New York State Joint Legislative Committee on Problems of the Aging. Legislative Document No. 12:49–51.

MEAD, M. 1967. The life cycle and its variation: The division of roles. Daedalus. Summer.

*MEYERS, T. 1966. The clitorid woman. Psychiat. Quart. 40(2): 248–257.

MILNER, E. 1949. Effects of sex roles and social status on the early adolescent personality. Gent. Psychol. Monogr. 40:235–325.

*MONEY, J., Ed. 1965. Sex Research. New Developments. Rinehart & Winston. New York, N. Y.

*NEISSER, E. 1967. Mothers and Daughters. Harper & Row. New York, N. Y.

POLLAK, O. & A. S. FRIEDMAN, Eds. Family Dynamics and Female Sexual Delinquency. Science and Behavior Books, Inc. Palo Alto, Calif.

RAINWATER, L., R. P. COLEMAN & G. HANDEL. 1959. Workingman's Wife: Her Personality, World and Life Style. Oceana Publ. New York, N. Y.

*REICH, W. 1942. The Function of the Orgasm. Orgone Institute Press. New York, N. Y.

REICH, W. 1945. The Sexual Revolution. Toward a Self-Governing Character Structure. Translated by T. P. Wolfe. Farrar, Straus & Giroux. New York, N. Y.

*REICH, W. 1961. Listen Little Man! Noonday Press. New York, N. Y.

REIK, T. 1949. Of Love and Lust. Farrar, Straus & Cudahy. New York, N. Y.

REIK, T. 1960. The Creation of Women. George Braziller. New York, N. Y.

*RHEINGOLD, J. C. 1964. The Fear of Being a Woman: A Theory of Maternal Destructiveness. Grune & Stratton. New York, N. Y.

*ROBINSON, M. 1959. The Power of Sexual Surrender. Doubleday & Co. New York, N. Y.

RODGERS, D. A., F. J. ZIEGLER, J. ALTROCCHI & N. LEVY. 1965. A longitudinal study of the psycho-social effects of vasectomy. J. Marr. Fam. 27:59—64.

ROHEIM, G. 1932. Psychoanalysis of primitive cultural types. Int. J. Psychoanal. 18.

ROSE, A. M. 1951. The adequacy of women's expectations for adult roles. Soc. Forces 30(1):69—77.

*ROSENFELS, P. 1966. Love and Power: The Psychology of Interpersonal Creativity. Libra.

*RUITENBEEK, H. M. 1962. The Male Myth. Dell Publ. Co. New York, N. Y.

*SALZMAN, L. 1967. Psychology of the female: A new look. Arch. Gen. Psychiat. 17:195—203.

*SAMPSON, R. V. 1965. The Psychology of Power. Pantheon Press. New York, N. Y.

*SANFORD, N., Ed. 1962. The American College. John Wiley & Sons, Inc. New York, N. Y.

*SANFORD, N. 1967. Self and Society: Social Change and Individual Development. Atherton Press. New York, N. Y.

SARLIN, C. N. 1963. Feminine identity. J. Amer. Psychoanal. Ass. 9:790—816.

*SCHEINFELD, A. 1944. Women and Men. Harcourt, Brace. New York, N. Y.

*SEWARD, G. H. 1946. Sex and the Social Order. McGraw-Hill Book Co. New York, N. Y.

SHERFEY, M. J. 1966. The evolution and nature of female sexuality in relation to psychoanalytic theory. J. Amer. Psychoanal. Ass. 14(1).

SHERMAN, J. A. 1967. Problem of sex differences in space perception and aspects of intellectual functioning. Psychol. Rev. 74(4):290—299.

*SKARD, A. G. 1967. Maternal deprivation: the research and its implications. J. Marr. Fam. 27(3).

SMITH, M. A. 1961. Compliance and defiance as it relates to role conflict in women. Diss. Abstr. 22(2):646.

*SOUBIRAN, A. 1968. Open Letter to a Woman of Today. James H. Heineman, Inc. New York, N. Y.

*STERN, K. 1965. The Flight from Woman. Noonday Press. New York, N. Y.

*STOLLER, R. J. 1968. Sex and Gender: On the Development of Masculinity and Femininity. Science House. New York, N. Y.

*STRECKER, E. 1946. Their Mother's Sons. Philadelphia, Pa.

SYSIHARJU, A. 1960. Equality, Home and Work: A Socio-Psychological Study on Finnish Student Women's Attitudes Toward the Woman's Role in Society. Mikkelissa. Helsinki, Finland.

TANGRI, S. S. 1969. Role-innovation in occupational choice. Doctoral dissertation. University of Michigan. Ann Arbor, Mich.

*TARBELL, I. The Ways of Woman. MacMillan & Co. New York, N. Y.

*TERMAN, L. & C. C. MILES. 1936. Sex and Personality: Studies in Masculinity and Femininity. McGraw-Hill Book Co. New York, N. Y.

THOMAS, W. I. 1967. The Unadjusted Girl (1923). Harper & Row. New York, N. Y.

*THOMPSON, H. B. 1903. The Mental Traits of Sex. University of Chicago Press. Chicago, Ill.

TORRANCE, E. P. 1960. Changing reactions of preadolescent girls to tasks requiring creative scientific thinking during a thirteen month period. In: New Educational Ideas. Proc. Third Minnesota Conf. Gifted Children.

TURNER, R. H. 1964. Some aspects of women's ambition. Amer. J. Sociol. 79(3):271–285.

*UESUGI, T. C. & W. E. VINACKE. 1963. Strategy in a feminine game. Sociometry 26:75–88.

VAERTUNG, M. & M. VAERTUNG. 1932. The Dominant Sex. A Study in the Sociology of Sex Differentiation. Allen & Unwin. London, England.

VANDEN BERG, J. H. 1961. The Changing Nature of Man. W. W. Norton. New York, N. Y.

VEROFF, J., S. WILCOX & J. W. ATKINSON. 1953. The achievement motive in high school and college age women. J. Abnorm. Soc. Psychol. 48:108–119.

WALLIN, P. 1950. Cultural contradictions and sex roles: A repeat study. Amer. Sociol. Rev. 15:288–293.

*WATTS, A. Nature, Man and Woman.

*WEININGER, O. 1966. Sex and Character. James H. Heineman, Inc. London, England.

WEISSTEIN, N. 1969. Woman as nigger. Psychol. Today. Oct.

ZISSUS, C. 1964. A study of the life planning of 550 freshman women at Purdue University. J. Nat. Ass. Wom. Deans Couns. 27(4): 153–159.

Female Physiology and Sexuality

*BALINT, A. 1937. Psychology of menstruation. Psychoanal. Quart. May.

BENEDEK, T. 1960. The organization of the reproductive drive. Int. J. Psychoanal. 41:1–15.

*BERGLER, E. & W. S. KROGER. 1954. Kinsey's Myth of Female Sexuality: The Medical Facts. Grune & Stratton. New York, N. Y.

*BLOCH, I. 1908. The Sexual Life of Our Time in Its Relation to Modern Civilization. London, England.

*BRECHER, R. & E. BRECHER. 1966. An Analysis of Human Sexual Response. New American Library. New York, N. Y.

*BULLOUGH, V. L. 1964. The History of Prostitution.

CALVERTON, V. F. & S. D. SCHMALHAUSEN. 1929. Sex in Civilization. MacCauley. New York, N. Y.

*CHADWICK, M. 1932. The Psychological Effects of Menstruation. Nervous and Mental Disease Pub. Co. New York, N. Y.

*COHN, D. L. 1943. Love in America, An Informal Study of Manners and Morals in American Marriage. Simon & Schuster. New York, N. Y.

*COWAN, J. 1869. The Science of a New Life. New York, N. Y.

*DITZION, S. 1953. Marriage, Morals and Sex in America – A History of Ideas. New York, N. Y.

ELLIS, A. 1955. The Folklore of Sex. New York, N. Y.

*ETZIONI, A. 1968. Sex control, science and society. Science. Sept. 13:1107–1112.

FORD, C. S. & F. A. BEACH. 1951. Patterns of Sexual Behavior. Harper Bros. New York, N. Y.

*GAGNON, J. H. 1965. Sexuality and sexual learning in the child. Psychiatry 8:212–228.

*GRAY, M. 1967. The Normal Woman. Scribner's. New York, N. Y.

*GREENWALD, H. The Call Girl.

*HALL, M. H. 1969. A conversation with Masters and Johnson. Psychol. Today 3(2):50–58.

*HEGELER, I. & S. HEGELER. 1963. An ABZ of Love. Translated by D. Hobner. Medical Press of New York. New York, N. Y.

*HENRIQUES, F. 1960. Love in Action: The Sociology of Sex. E. P. Dutton & Co. New York, N. Y.

*HENRIQUES, F. 1961. Stew and Strumpets: A Survey of Prostitution. MacGibbon & Kee. London, England.

*HENRIQUES, F. 1962. Prostitution in Europe and the Americas.

*HIRSCH, A. H. 1963. The Love Elite. (The Story of Woman's Emancipation and Her Drive for Sexual Fulfillment). Julian Press. New York, N. Y.

*HUNT, M. 1962. Her Infinite Variety: The American Woman as Lover, Rival, and Mate.

*KINSEY, A. C. 1963. Sexual Behavior in the Human Female. W. B. Saunders Co. Philadelphia, Pa.

*KRONHAUSEN, P. & E. KRONHAUSEN. The Sexually Responsive Female.

MALINOWSKI, B. 1927. Sex and Repression in Savage Society. The Humanities Press. New York, N. Y.

MALINOWSKI, B. 1962. Sex, Culture and Myth. Harcourt Brace & World, New York, N. Y.

*MARCUSE, H. 1955. Eros and Civilization. Beacon Press. New York, N. Y.

*MASTERS, W. H. & V. E. JOHNSON. 1966. Human Sexual Response. Little, Brown & Co. Boston, Mass.

MASTERS, W. H. & V. E. JOHNSON. 1970. Human Sexual Inadequacy. Little, Brown & Co. Boston, Mass.

*MEAD, M. 1935. Sex and Temperament in Three Primitive Societies. William Morrow & Co. New York, N. Y.

*MEAD, M. 1949. Male and Female. William Morrow & Co. New York, N. Y.

MEAD, M. 1961. Cultural determinants of sexual behavior. In: Sex and Internal Secretions. W. C. Young, Ed. 3rd edit. 2:1433–1479. The Williams & Wilkins Co. Baltimore, Md.

*MONTAGUE, A. The Natural Superiority of Women.

*MONEY, J., Ed. 1965. Sex Research. New Developments. Rinehart & Winston. New York, N. Y.

*REICH, W. 1965. The Sexual Revolution. Farrar, Straus & Giroux. New York, N. Y.

RODGERS, D. A., F. J. ZIEGLER, J. ALTROCCHI & N. LEVY. 1965. A longitudinal study of the psycho-social effects of vasectomy. J. Marr. Fam. 27:59–64.

*SCHEINFELD, A. 1944. Women and Men. Harcourt, Brace. New York, N. Y.

*STOLLER, R. J. 1968. Sex and Gender: On the Development of Masculinity and Femininity. Science House. New York, N. Y.

*TARBELL, I. The Ways of Woman. MacMillan & Co. New York, N. Y.

*TAYLOR, G. R. 1953. Sex in History. Thames & Hudson. London, England.

THIESSEN, D. D. & D. A. RODGERS. 1961. Population density and endocrine function. Psychol. Bull. 58:441–451.

TIETZE, C. 1962. Surgical Sterilization of Men and Women: A Selected Bibliography. National Committee on Maternal Health. New York, N. Y.

*WATTS, A. Nature, Man, and Woman.

*WEININGER, O. 1966. Sex and Character. James H. Heineman, Inc. London, England.

*WULFFEN, E. 1935. Woman as a Sexual Criminal. Falstaff Press. New York, N. Y.

*YOUNG, W. Eros Denied: Sex in Western Society. Grove Press. New York, N. Y.

Related Social Commentary

*BELL, D., Ed. 1968. Toward the year 2,000: Work in Progress. Houghton-Mifflin. Boston, Mass.

*BELLAMY, E. Looking Backward.

*De RHAM, E. 1969. How Could She Do That? Clarkson Potter. New York, N. Y.

FISHMAN, K. D. 1966. Children at stake. N. Y. Times Mag. Dec. 11.

*HAWES, E. 1939. Men Can Take It. Random House. New York, N. Y.

*HAWES, E. 1943. Why Women Cry, or, Wenches with Wrenches. Reynal & Hitchcock. New York, N. Y.

*LYNES, R. 1963. The Domesticated Americans. Harper & Row. New York, N. Y.

*MANNES, M. More in Anger.

*MARCUSE, H. 1964. One-Dimensional Man. Beacon Press. New York, N. Y.

*MAY, E. 1964. The Wasted Americans. New York, N. Y.

*McLUHAN, H. M. 1951. The Mechanical Bride.

*McLUHAN, H. M. 1964. Understanding Media.

MEAD, M. 1962. Introduction. In: American Women: The Changing Image. B. B. CASSARA, Ed.:ix-xv. Beacon Press. Boston, Mass.

MEAD, M. & F. B. KAPLAN, Eds. 1965. Epilogue. In: American Women.:181–204. Scribner & Sons. New York, N. Y.

MEAD, M. 1969. The American Woman today. In: The 1969 World Book Year Book.:78–95. Field Enterprises Educational Corporation. Chicago, Ill.

MEZERIK, A. C. 1945. Getting rid of the women. Atlantic Monthly. June.

*MONTAGUE, A. The Natural Superiority of Women.

*SMITH, L. Killers of the Dream.

STERN, E. M. 1949. Women are household slaves. Amer. Mercury. Jan.

THURBER, J. & E. B. WHITE. 1964. Is Sex Necessary? Dell Publ. Co. New York, N. Y.

*WINICk, C. 1968. The New People.

*WYLIE, P. Generation of Vipers.

General Works: Historical, Philosophical, Religious, Anthropological, and Sociological

*ADAMS, M. 1967. The Right to be People. J. B. Lippincott Co. Philadelphia, Pa.

*ANTHONY, S. B., E. C. STANTON & I. H. HARPER. History of Women's Suffrage.

BACHOFEN, J. J. 1967. Myth, Religion and Mother Right. Bollinger Series. Princeton, N. J.

*BARDECHE, M. 1969. History of Women.

*BEARD, M. 1931. On Understanding Women. Longmans, Green & Co. London, England.

*BEARD, M. 1946. Women as Force in History.

*BELFORT BAX, E. 1913. The Fraud of Feminism. Grant Richards. London, England.

*"MARGARET BENNETT" (pseud.). The Feminine Mistake, or, Alice in Womanland.

*BETTELHEIM, B. 1962. Symbolic Wounds: Puberty Rites and the Envious Male. P. F. Collier, Inc. New York, N. Y.

*BRITTAIN, V. 1953. Lady into Women: A History of Women from Victoria to Elizabeth II. MacMillan & Co. New York, N. Y.

*BROWN, M. M. 1962. The Secret Life of Jeanne D'Arc. Vantage Press. New York, N. Y.

*CALLAHAN, S. 1965. The Illusion of Eve. Sheed & Ward. New York, N. Y.

*CARROL, M. Prolegomena to the Study of Greek Religions.

*CASH, W. J. 1941. The Mind of the South. New York, N. Y.

CHERNYSHEVDKY, N. G. 1863. What is to be Done? Russia.

*COX, H. 1965. The Secular City. MacMillan & Co. New York, N. Y.

CRAWLEY, E. 1927. The Mystic Rose. Methuen. London, England.

*DALY, M. 1968. The Church and the Second Sex. Harper & Row. New York, N. Y.

*DANGERFIELD, G. 1961. The Strange Death of Liberal England, 1910–1914. Capricorn Books. New York, N. Y.

*DEGLER, C. N. 1958. Out of Our Past.

*De ROUGEMONT, D. 1956. Love in the Western World. Pantheon Press. New York, N. Y.

*DINER, H. 1965. Mothers and Amazons: The First Feminine History of Culture. Julian Press. New York, N. Y.

*DOLLARD, J. 1937. The sexual gain. In: Caste and Class in a Southern Town.

*DRINKER, S. Music and Women.

*DUNN, N. 1965. Talking to Women.

*DURKHEIM, E. Suicide.

*EATON, C. Freedom of Thought in the South.

*FAWCETT, M. G. 1912. Women's Suffrage. The People's Books. London, England.

*FLEXNER, E. 1966. Century of Struggle: The Woman's Rights Movement in the United States. Belknap Press, Harvard University. Cambridge, Mass.

FULFORD, 1957. Votes for Women. Farber & Farber. London, England.

FURNESS, C. F. 1931. The Genteel Female, An Anthology. Alfred A. Knopf. New York, N. Y.

GANS, H. 1962. The Urban Villagers. The Free Press. New York, N. Y.

GANS, H. 1967. The Levittowners.

GAVRON, H. 1966. The Captive Wife. Routledge & Kegan Paul. London, England.

*GILMAN, C. P. 1898. Women and Economics. Charlton Co., New York, N. Y.

*GILMAN, C. P. 1914. The Man-Made World: Our Androcentric Culture. Charlton Co. New York, N. Y.

GOLDBERG, D. 1963. The Creative Woman. David McKay Co. New York, N. Y.

*GOODMAN, P. & P. GOODMAN. 1944. Communitas.

*GOODWIN, M., Ed. 1951. Nineteenth Century Opinion. Pelican Books. New York, N. Y.

GRAHAM, A. 1934. Ladies in Revolt. The Woman's Press. New York, N. Y.

GRIMES, A. P. 1967. The Puritan Ethic and Woman Suffrage. Oxford University Press. New York, N. Y.

*GRIMKE, A. Appeal to the Christian Women of the South.

*GRIMKE, S. Letters on Equality of the Sexes.

*HACKER, H. 1951. Women as a minority group. Soc. Forces. 30:60–69.

*HAGOOD, M. 1939. Mothers of the South. University of North Carolina Press. Chapel Hill, N. C.

*HALL, E. T. 1963. The Silent Language. Premier Books. New York, N. Y.

*HARDING, E. 1955. Woman's Mysteries. Pantheon Press. New York, N. Y.

*HAWES, E. 1948. Anything but Love. Rinehart Publ. Co. New York, N. Y.

*HAYS, H. R. 1964. The Dangerous Sex, The Myth of Feminine Evil. G. P. Putnam. New York, N. Y.

*HENRY, J. Culture Against Man.

*HERNTON, C. C. 1965. Sex and Racism in America. Grove Press. New York, N. Y.

*HIMMELFARB, G. 1968. Victorian Minds. Weidenfeld-Nicholson. London, England.

*HINDS, W. A. 1961. American Communities. Corinth Books. New York, N. Y.

*HINTON, W. 1966. Fan-Shen. Random House. New York, N. Y.

*IRWIN, I. H. 1934. Angels and Amazons: 100 Years of American Women.

*IRWIN, I. H. 1934. The Story of the Woman's Party. New York, N. Y.

*JACOBS, J. 1961. The Death and Life of Great American Cities. New York, N. Y.

*KENNEDY, R. W. 1953. The House and the Art of Its Design. Reinhold Publ. Co. New York, N. Y.

*KIRA, A. 1966. The Bathroom: Criteria for Design. Cornell University Press. Ithaca, N. Y.

*KLEIN, V. 1946. The Feminine Character, History of an Ideology. Kegan Paul. London, England.

*KRADITOR, A. 1965. The Ideas of the Woman Suffrage Movement, 1890–1920. Columbia University Press. New York, N. Y.

*KRADITOR, A. 1968. Up From the Pedestal, Landmark Writings in the American Woman's Struggle for Equality. Quadrangle Books. Chicago, Ill.

*LAMB, F. & H. PICKTHORN. 1968. Locked-Up Daughters. Hodder-Stoughton. London, England.

*LASCH, C. The New Radicalism in America, 1889–1963.

*LEONARD, E. A. 1965. The Dear-Bought Heritage. University of Pennsylvania Press. Philadelphia, Pa.

LEONARD, E. A., S. H. DRINKER & M. Y. HOLDEN. 1962. The American Woman in Colonial and Revolutionary Times, 1565–1800. University of Pennsylvania Press. Philadelphia, Pa.

LERNER, G. 1966. Changes in the status of women: 1800–1840. Paper, read at the American Historical Association Meeting, Dec.

LEWIS, F. 1967. The femininity thing. N. Y. Post. April 17.

*LUDOVICI, L. J. 1965. The Final Inequality. W. W. Norton. New York, N. Y.

*LUTZ, A. 1968. Crusade for Freedom: Women in the Antislavery Movement. Beacon Press. New York, N. Y.

*MARCUS, S. 1966. The Other Victorians: A Study of Sexuality and Pornography in Mid-Nineteenth Century England. Basic Books. New York, N. Y.

*MARTINEAU, H. 1837. Society in America. (2 vols.) Saunders & Otley. New York, N. Y.

McGREGOR, O. 1955. The social position of women in England 1850–1914: A bibliography. Brit. J. Sociol. March.

McLENNON, J. 1885. The Patriarchal Theory. MacMillan & Co. London, England.

MEAD, M. 1940. The arts in Bali. Yale Rev. 30(2):335–347.

*MEAD, M. 1943. And Keep Your Powder Dry. William Morrow & Co. New York, N. Y.

*MEAD, M. 1966. The case for drafting all boys – and girls. Redbook. Sept.

*MENCKEN, H. L. 1922. In Defense of Women. Alfred A. Knopf. New York, N. Y.

*MERRIAM, E. After Nora Slammed the Door.

MILL, J. S. 1966. The Subjection of Women (1869). Oxford University Press. London, England.

*MYRDAL, G. 1944. An American Dilemma. (2 vols.) Harper Bros. New York, N. Y.

*NEVINSON, M. 1911. Ancient Suffragettes.

*O'MEARA, W. 1968. Daughters of the Country: The Women of the Furtraders and Mountain Men. Harcourt, Brace & World. New York, N. Y.

*O'NEILL, W. L. 1968. Feminism as a radical ideology. In: Dissent: Explorations in the History of American Radicalism. A. E. Young, Ed.:273—300. Northern Illinois University Press. De Kalb, Ill.

O'NEILL, W. L. 1969. Everyone was Brave, the Rise and Fall of Feminism in America. Quadrangle Books. Chicago, Ill.

*PACKARD, V. The Hidden Persuaders.

*PACKARD, V. 1968. The Sexual Wilderness: The Contemporary Upheaval in Male-Female Relationships. David McKay Co. New York, N. Y.

PANKHURST, E. 1914. My Own Story, Everleigh Nash. London, England.

*PANKHURST, S. 1931. The Suffragette Movement. Longmans, Green & Co. New York, N. Y.

PARSONS, T. 1954. Age and sex in the social structure of the United States. In: Essays in Sociological Theory. The Free Press. Glencoe, Ill.

PUTNAM, E. J. 1970. The Lady: Studies of Certain Significant Phases of Her History (1910). The University of Chicago Press. Chicago, Ill.

*RAINWATER, L. & W. L. YANCEY. 1967. The Moynihan Report and the Politics of Controversy. Massachusetts Institute of Technology Press. Cambridge, Mass.

*RAMELSON, M. The Petticoat Rebellion.

*REID, M. 1848. Woman, Her Education and Influence. New York, N. Y.

REYNOLDS, M. 1920. The Learned Lady in England, 1650—1760. Houghton-Mifflin. Boston, Mass.

ROESCH, R. 1967. Women in Action — Their Questions and Their Answers. John Day Co. New York, N. Y.

*ROGERS, K. M. 1966. The Troublesome Helpmate. A History of Misogyny in Literature. University of Washington Press. Seattle, Wash.

RUBIN, T. I. 1961. In the Life. MacMillan & Co. New York, N. Y.

RUSKIN, J. 1902. Of queens gardens. In: Sesame and Lilies. Homewood. Chicago, Ill.

*RUSSELL, D. 1925. Hypatia, or, Woman and Knowledge. E. P. Dutton & Co. New York, N. Y.

SCOTT, A. F. 1964. After suffrage: Southern women in the 1920's. J. Soc. Hist. 30:298—318.

*SILLEN, S. 1955. Women Against Slavery. Masses & Mainstream. New York, N. Y.

*SINCLAIR, A. 1965. The Emancipation of the American Woman. Harper & Row. New York, N. Y.

*SPRAGUE, W. 1940. Women and the West. Boston, Mass.

*STAMPP, K. The Peculiar Institution.

*STEVENS, D. Jailed for Freedom.

STRACHEY, R. 1928. The Cause: A Short History of the Woman's Movement in Great Britain. G. Bell & Sons. London, England.

*TAVES, I. 1968. Women Alone. Funk & Wagnalls. New York, N. Y.

TEMPERLEY, H. W. V. 1925. The sale of wives in England in 1823. The History Teacher's Miscellany 3:66.

*THEOBALD, R., *et al.* 1967. Dialogue on Women. Bobbs-Merrill. Indianapolis, Ind.

THOMAS, C. 1943. Women in Nazi Germany. Gollancz. London, England.

THOMAS, E. 1966. The Women Incendiaries. Goerge Braziller. New York, N. Y.

*THOMAS, W. I. 1907. Sex and Society. Richard G. Badger. Boston, Mass.

*THOMPSON, W. 1825. Appeal of One Half of the Human Race, Women, Against the Pretensions of the Other Half, Men. London, England.

TIGER, L. 1969. Men in Groups. Random House. New York, N. Y.

*TURNER, E. S. 1955. A History of Courting. E. P. Dutton & Co. New York, N. Y.

*WAKEFIELD, D. 1968. Supernation at Peace and War. (Atlantic) Little, Brown & Co.

WALSH, C. M. 1917. Feminism. Sturgis & Watton. New York, N. Y.

*WIETH-KNUDSEN, K. A. 1928. Feminism, a Sociological Study of the Woman Question from Ancient Times to Present Day. Constable. London, England.

*WOLLSTONECRAFT, M. 1792. A Vindication of the Rights of Women.

*WOODWARD, H. 1960. The Lady Persuaders. New York, N. Y.

*WOODY, T. H. 1929. A History of Women's Education in the United States. (2 vol.)

*WOOLF, V. 1929. A Room of One's Own. Harcourt, Brace & World. New York, N. Y.

*WOOLF, V. 1938. Three Guineas. Harcourt, Brace & World. New York, N. Y.

CONTRIBUTORS

Margaret Adams is a consultant in social work at the Eunice Kennedy Shriver Center of the Fernald School in Waverley, Massachusetts, teaches family counseling at the Lesley College Graduate Center, and is a faculty member of the Cambridge-Goddard Graduate School for Social Change. Her most recent book is *Mental Retardation and Its Social Dimensions.*

Janet Zollinger Giele taught at Wellesley College before becoming a Fellow and then Senior Fellow at the Radcliffe Institute in Cambridge, Massachusetts.

Miriam G. Keiffer is a Professor of Psychology who has been associated with the Educational Testing Service in Princeton, New Jersey and with the Bensalem Experimental College in the Bronx, New York.

Zelda S. Klapper is an Associate Professor of Pediatrics and Chief of Psychological Services in the Children's Evaluation and Rehabilitation Clinic at the Rose F. Kennedy Center of the Albert Einstein College of Medicine.

Birgitta Linnér is a Family Life Education Consultant at the Municipal Family Guidance Clinic in Stockholm, Sweden. A member of several national and international groups concerned with family planning and education, she is also the author of *Sex and Society in Sweden.*

Margaret Mead is Curator Emeritus of Ethnology at the American Museum of Natural History.

Jean Baker Miller is a practicing psychoanalyst who is also a Clinical Assistant Professor of Psychiatry at the Albert Einstein College of Medicine.

Ira Mothner is currently an Assistant to Mayor John V. Lindsay of New York City. A former Senior Editor of *Look,* he is co-author of the recent book, *Drugs, Parents and Children: The Three-Way Connection.*

Mordeca Jane Pollock, an Assistant Professor of French at Brandeis University, was the founding president of the Eastern Massachusetts Chapter of the National Organization for Women (NOW). She serves as a member of NOW's National Board of Directors and its Legal Defense and Education Fund.

Clara Rabinowitz is a psychologist at the New York Medical College and has been a member of the Editorial Board of the *American Journal of Orthopsychiatry* since 1962.

Catherine Kohler Riessman is a member of the staff at the Mental Hygiene Clinic at the Albert Einstein College of Medicine in the Bronx, New York.

Ethel Tobach is Curator of the Department of Animal Behavior at The American Museum of Natural History and an Adjunct Professor at the City College of New York and at Hunter College. She also participated in the formation of the Association for Women in Psychology.

Tomannie T. Walker is Director of Case Work Services at the League for Seriously Disturbed Children in Brooklyn, New York.

Patricia A. Warren is a Senior Research Assistant with the Educational Testing Service in Princeton, New Jersey.

Helen Wortis has been a member of the Editorial Board of the *American Journal of Orthopsychiatry* since 1962. She has also served on the faculties of the Downstate Medical College and New York Medical College.

Rochelle Paul Wortis, also known as Sheli Wortis, teaches in the Feminist Studies Program at the Cambridge-Goddard Graduate School in Massachusetts. She has been active in the Women's Liberation Movement since 1969.

A Note about This Book

The text of this book was set on an IBM Selectric Composer System in the type face, Press Roman. The book was composed by dcmj typesetting, New York and was printed and bound by Braun & Brumfield, Ann Arbor, Michigan. Production design by diz, Donald Mowbray, Thomas F. Wolf, and Harry Segessman. The cover for the paperback edition of this book was designed by Donald Mowbray.